A CHICAGO PRINCESS

"The twinkling eyes of the Emperor fixed themselves on Miss Hemster."

A CHICAGO PRINCESS

By ROBERT BARR

Author of "Over the Border," "The Victors," "Tekla,"
"In the Midst of Alarms," "A Woman Intervenes," etc.

Illustrated by FRANCIS P. WIGHTMAN

WILDSIDE PRESS

A CHICAGO PRINCESS

CHAPTER I

W HEN I look back upon a certain hour of my
life it fills me with wonder that I should
have been so peacefully happy. Strange
as it may seem, utter despair is not without its alloy of
joy. The man who daintily picks his way along a
muddy street is anxious lest he soil his polished boots,
or turns up his coat collar to save himself from the
shower that is beginning, eager then to find a shelter;
but let him inadvertently step into a pool, plunging
head over ears into foul water, and after that he has no
more anxiety. Nothing that weather can inflict will
add to his misery, and consequently a ray of happiness
illumines his gloomy horizon. He has reached the
limit; Fate can do no more; and there is a satisfaction
in attaining the ultimate of things. So it was with me
that beautiful day; I had attained my last phase.

I was living in the cheapest of all paper houses, living as the Japanese themselves do, on a handful of
rice, and learning by experience how very little it requires to keep body and soul together. But now, when
I had my next meal of rice, it would be at the expense

I

of my Japanese host, who was already beginning to suspect,—so it seemed to me,—that 1 might be unable to liquidate whatever debt I incurred. He was very polite about it, but in his twinkling little eyes there lurked suspicion. I have travelled the whole world over, especially the East, and I find it the same everywhere. When a man comes down to his final penny, some subtle change in his deportment seems to make the whole world aware of it. But then, again, this supposed knowledge on the part of the world may have existed only in my own imagination, as the Christian Scientists tell us every ill resides in the mind. Perhaps, after all, my little bowing landlord was not troubling himself about the payment of the bill, and I only fancied him uneasy.

If an untravelled person, a lover of beauty, were sitting in my place on that little elevated veranda, it is possible the superb view spread out before him might account for serenity in circumstances which to the ordinary individual would be most depressing. But the view was an old companion of mine; goodness knows I had looked at it often enough when I climbed that weary hill and gazed upon the town below me, and the magnificent harbor of Nagasaki spreading beyond. The water was intensely blue, dotted with shipping of all nations, from the stately men-of-war to the ocean tramps and the little coasting schooners. It was an ever-changing, animated scene; but really I had had enough of it during all those ineffective months of struggle in the attempt to earn even the rice and the poor lodging which I enjoyed.

A CHICAGO PRINCESS

Curiously, it was not of this harbor I was thinking, but of another in far-distant Europe, that of Boulogne in the north of France, where I spent a day with my own yacht before I sailed for America. And it was a comical thought that brought the harbor of Boulogne to my mind. I had seen a street car there, labelled "Le Dernier Sou," which I translated as meaning "The Last Cent." I never took a trip on this street car, but I presume somewhere in the outskirts of Boulogne there is a suburb named "The Last Cent," and I thought now with a laugh: "Here I am in Japan, and although I did not take that street car, yet I have arrived at 'Le Dernier Sou.'"

This morning I had not gone down to the harbor to prosecute my search for employment. As with my last cent, I had apparently given that idea up. There was no employer needing men to whom I had not applied time and again, willing to take the laborer's wage for the laborer's work. But all my earlier training had been by way of making me a gentleman, and the manner was still upon me in spite of my endeavors to shake it off, and I had discovered that business men do not wish gentlemen as day-laborers. There was every reason that I should be deeply depressed; yet, strange to say, I was not. Had I at last reached the lotus-eating content of the vagabond? Was this care-free condition the serenity of the tramp? Would my next step downward be the unblushing begging of food, with the confidence that if I were refused at one place I should receive at another? With later knowledge, looking back at that moment of mitigated happiness, I am forced to believe that it was the effect of coming events casting their shadows before. Some occultists tell us that every action that takes place on the earth, no matter how secretly done, leaves its impression on some ethereal atmosphere, visible to a clairvoyant, who can see and describe to us exactly what has taken place. If this be true, it is possible that our future experiences may give sub-mental warnings of their approach.

As I sat there in the warm sunlight and looked over the crowded harbor, I thought of the phrase, " When my ship comes in." There was shipping enough in the bay, and possibly, if I could but have known where, some friend of mine might at that moment be tramping a white deck, or sitting in a steamer chair, looking up at terrace upon terrace of the toy houses among which I kept my residence. Perhaps my ship had come in already if only I knew which were she. As I lay back on the light bamboo chair, along which I had thrown myself,— a lounging, easy, half-reclining affair like those we used to have at college,— I gazed upon the lower town and harbor, taking in the vast blue surface of the bay; and there along the indigo expanse of the waters, in striking contrast to them, floated a brilliantly white ship gradually, imperceptibly approaching. The canvas, spread wing and wing, as it increased in size, gave it the appearance of a swan swimming toward me, and I thought lazily:

" It is like a dove coming to tell me that my deluge of misery is past, and there is an olive-branch of foam in its beak."

As the whole ship became visible I saw that it, like

4

the canvas, was pure white, and at first I took it for a large sailing yacht rapidly making Nagasaki before the gentle breeze that was blowing; but as she drew near I saw that she was a steamer, whose trim lines, despite her size, were somewhat unusual in these waters. If this were indeed a yacht she must be owned by some man of great wealth, for she undoubtedly cost a fortune to build and a very large income to maintain. As she approached the more crowded part of the bay, her sails were lowered and she came slowly in on her own momentum. I fancied I heard the rattle of the chain as her anchor plunged into the water, and now I noticed with a thrill that made me sit up in my lounging chair that the flag which flew at her stern was the Stars and Stripes. It is true that I had little cause to be grateful to the country which this piece of bunting represented, for had it not looted me of all I possessed? Nevertheless in those distant regions an Englishman regards the United States flag somewhat differently from that of any nation save his own. Perhaps there is an unconscious feeling of kinship; perhaps the similarity of language may account for it, because an Englishman understands American better than any other foreign tongue. Be that as it may, the listlessness departed from me as I gazed upon that banner, as crude and gaudy as our own, displaying the most striking of the primary colors. The yacht rested on the blue waters as gracefully as if she were a large white waterfowl, and I saw the sampans swarm around her like a fluffy brood of ducklings.

And now I became conscious that the most polite individual in the world was making an effort to secure my attention, yet striving to accomplish his purpose in the most unobtrusive way. My patient and respected landlord, Yansan, was making deep obeisances before me, and he held in his hand a roll which I strongly suspected to be my overdue bill. I had the merit in Yansan's eyes of being able to converse with him in his own language, and the further advantage to myself of being able to read it; therefore he bestowed upon me a respect which he did not accord to all Europeans.

"Ah, Yansan!" I cried to him, taking the bull by the horns, "I was just thinking of you. I wish you would be more prompt in presenting your account. By such delay errors creep into it which I am unable to correct."

Yansan awarded me three bows, each lower than the one preceding it, and, while bending his back, endeavored, though with some confusion, to conceal the roll in his wide sleeve. Yansan was possessed of much shrewdness, and the bill certainly was a long standing one.

"Your Excellency," he began, "confers too much honor on the dirt beneath your feet by mentioning the trivial sum that is owing. Nevertheless, since it is your Excellency's command, I shall at once retire and prepare the document for you."

"Oh, don't trouble about that, Yansan," I said, "just pull it out of your sleeve and let me look over it."

The wrinkled face screwed itself up into a grimace more like that of a monkey than usual, and so, with various genuflections, Yansan withdrew the roll and proffered it to me. Therein, in Japanese characters, was set down the long array of my numerous debts to him. Now, in whatever part of the world a man wishes to delay the payment of a bill, the proper course is to dispute one or more of its items, and this accordingly I proceeded to do.

"I grieve to see, Yansan," I began, putting my finger on the dishonest hieroglyphic, "that on the fourth day you have set down against me a repast of rice, whereas you very well know on that occasion I did myself the honor to descend into the town and lunch with his Excellency the Governor."

Again Yansan lowered his ensign three times, then deplored the error into which he had fallen, saying it would be immediately rectified.

"There need to be no undue hurry about the rectification," I replied, "for when it comes to a settlement I shall not be particular about the price of a plate of rice."

Yansan was evidently much gratified to hear this, but I could see that my long delay in liquidating his account was making it increasingly difficult for him to subdue his anxiety. The fear of monetary loss was struggling with his native politeness. Then he used the formula which is correct the world over.

"Excellency, I am a poor man, and next week have heavy payments to make to a creditor who will put me in prison if I produce not the money."

"Very well," said I grandly, waving my hand toward the crowded harbor, "my ship has come in where you see the white against the blue. To-morrow you shall be paid."

Yansan looked eagerly in the direction of my gesture.

" She is English," he said.

" No, American."

" It is a war-ship? "

" No, she belongs to a private person, not to the Government."

" Ah, he must be a king, then,— a king of that country."

" Not so, Yansan; he is one of many kings, a pork king, or an oil king or a railroad king."

" Surely there cannot be but one king in a country, Excellency," objected Yansan.

" Ah, you are thinking of a small country like Japan. One king does for such a country; but America is larger than many Japans, therefore it has numerous kings, and here below us is one of them."

" I should think, Excellency," said Yansan, " that they would fight with one another."

" That they do, and bitterly, too, in a way your kings never thought of. I myself was grievously wounded in one of their slightest struggles. That flag which you see there waves over my fortune. Many a million of sen pieces which once belonged to me rest secure for other people under its folds."

My landlord lifted his hands in amazement at my immense wealth.

" This, then, is perhaps the treasure-ship bringing money to your Excellency," he exclaimed, awestricken.

8

"That's just what it is, Yansan, and I must go down and collect it; so bring me a dinner of rice, that I may be prepared to meet the captain who carries my fortune."

CHAPTER II

AFTER a frugal repast I went down the hill to the lower town, and on inquiry at the custom-house learned that the yacht was named the " Michigan," and that she was owned by Silas K. Hemster, of Chicago. So far as I could learn, the owner had not come ashore; therefore I hired a sampan from a boatman who trusted me. I was already so deeply in his debt that he was compelled to carry me, inspired by the optimistic hope that some day the tide of my fortunes would turn. I believe that commercial institutions are sometimes helped over a crisis in the same manner, as they owe so much their creditors dare not let them sink. Many a time had this lad ferried me to one steamer after another, until now his anxiety that I should obtain remunerative employment was nearly as great as my own.

As we approached the " Michigan " I saw that a rope ladder hung over the side, and there leaned against the rail a very free-and-easy sailor in white duck, who was engaged in squirting tobacco-juice into Nagasaki Bay. Intuitively I understood that he had sized up the city of Nagasaki and did not think much of it. Probably it compared unfavorably with Chicago. The seaman made no opposition to my mounting the ladder;

in fact he viewed my efforts with the greatest indifference. Approaching him, I asked if Mr. Hemster was aboard, and with a nod of his head toward the after part of the vessel he said, "That's him."

Looking aft, I now noticed a man sitting in a cushioned cane chair, with his two feet elevated on the spotless rail before him. He also was clothed in light summer garb, and had on his head a somewhat disreputable slouch hat with a very wide brim. His back was toward Nagasaki, as if he had no interest in the place. He revolved an unlit cigar in his mouth, in a manner quite impossible to describe; but as I came to know him better I found that he never lit his weed, but kept its further end going round and round in a little circle by a peculiar motion of his lips. Though he used the very finest brand of cigars, none ever lasted him for more than ten minutes, when he would throw it away, take another, bite off the end, and go through the same process once more. What satisfaction he got out of an unlighted cigar I was never able to learn.

His was a thin, keen, business face, with no hair on it save a tuft at the chin, like the beard of a goat. As I approached him I saw that he was looking sideways at me out of the corners of his eyes, but he neither raised his head nor turned it around. I was somewhat at a loss how to greet him, but for want of a better opening I began:

"I am told you are Mr. Hemster."

"Well!" he drawled slowly, with his cigar between his teeth, released for a moment from the circular movement of his lips, "you may thank your stars you are told something you can believe in this God-for-saken land."

I smiled at this unexpected reply and ventured:

"As a matter of fact, the East is not renowned for its truthfulness. I know it pretty well."

"You do, eh? Do you understand it?"

"I don't think either an American or a European ever understands an Asiatic people."

"Oh, yes, we do," rejoined Mr. Hemster; "they're liars and that's all there is *to* them. Liars and lazy; that sums them up."

As I was looking for the favor of work, it was not my place to contradict him, and the confident tone in which he spoke showed that contradiction would have availed little. He was evidently one of the men who knew it all, and success had confirmed him in his belief. I had met people of his calibre before,—to my grief.

"Well, young man, what can I do for you?" he asked, coming directly to the point.

"I am looking for a job," I said.

"What's your line?"

"I beg your pardon?"

"What can you do?"

"I am capable of taking charge of this ship as captain, or of working as a man before the mast."

"You spread yourself out too thin, my son. A man who can do everything can do nothing. We specialize in our country. I hire men who can do only one thing, and do that thing better than anybody else."

"Sir, I do not agree with you," I could not help

saying. "The most capable people in the world are the Americans. The best log house I ever saw was built by a man who owned a brown-stone front on Fifth Avenue. He simply pushed aside the guides whose specialty it was to do such things, took the axe in his own hands, and showed them how it should be accomplished."

Mr. Hemster shoved his hat to the back of his head, and for the first time during our interview looked me squarely in the face.

"Where was that?" he inquired.

"Up in Canada."

"Oh, well, the Fifth Avenue man had probably come from the backwoods and so knew how to handle an axe."

"It's more than likely," I admitted.

"What were you doing in Canada?"

"Fishing and shooting."

"You were n't one of the guides he pushed aside?"

I laughed.

"No, I was one of the two who paid for the guides."

"Well, to come back to first principles," continued Mr. Hemster, "I've got a captain who gives me perfect satisfaction, and he hires the crew. What else can you do?"

"I am qualified to take a place as engineer if your present man is n't equally efficient with the captain; and I can guarantee to give satisfaction as a stoker, although I don't yearn for the job."

"My present engineer I got in Glasgow," said Mr. Hemster; "and as for stokers we have a mechanical stoker which answers the purpose reasonably well, although I have several improvements I am going to patent as soon as I get home. I believe the Scotchman I have as engineer is the best in the business. I would n't interfere with him for the world."

My heart sank, and I began to fear that Yansan and the sampan-boy would have to wait longer for their money. It seemed that it was n't my ship that had come in, after all.

"Very well, Mr. Hemster," I said, "I must congratulate you on being so well suited. I am much obliged to you for receiving me so patiently without a letter of introduction on my part, and so I bid you good-day."

I turned for the ladder, but Mr. Hemster said, with more of animation in his tone than he had hitherto exhibited:

" Wait a moment, sonny; don't be so hasty. You 've asked me a good many questions about the yacht and the crew, so I should like to put some to you, and who knows but we may make a deal yet. There 's the galley and the stewards, and that sort of thing, you know. Draw up a chair and sit down."

I did as I was requested. Mr. Hemster threw his cigar overboard and took out another. Then he held out the case toward me, saying:

" Do you smoke?"

" Thank you," said I, selecting a cigar.

" Have you matches?" he asked, " I never carry them myself."

" No, I have n't," I admitted.

14

He pushed a button near him, and a Japanese steward appeared.

" Bring a box of matches and a bottle of champagne," he said.

The steward set a light wicker table at my elbow, disappeared for a few minutes, and shortly returned with a bottle of champagne and a box of matches. Did my eyes deceive me, or was this the most noted brand in the world, and of the vintage of '78? It seemed too good to be true.

" Would you like a sandwich or two with that wine, or is it too soon after lunch? "

" I could do with a few sandwiches," I confessed, thinking of Yansan's frugal fare; and shortly after there were placed before me, on a dainty, white, linen-and-lace-covered plate, some of the most delicious chicken sandwiches that it has ever been my fortune to taste.

" Now," said Mr. Hemster, when the steward had disappeared, " you 're on your uppers, I take it."

" I don't think I understand."

" Why, you 're down at bed-rock. Have n't you been in America? Don't you know the language? "

" 'Yes ' is the answer to all your questions."

" What 's the reason? Drink? Gambling? "

Lord, how good that champagne tasted! I laughed from the pure, dry exhilaration of it.

" I wish I could say it was drink that brought me to this pass," I answered; " for this champagne shows it would be a tempting road to ruin. I am not a gambler, either. How I came to this pass would not interest you."

"Well, I take it that 's just an Englishman's way of saying it 's none of my business; but such is not the fact. You want a job, and you have come to me for it. Very well; I must know something about you. Whether I can give you a job or not will depend. You have said you could captain the ship or run her engines. What makes you so confident of your skill?"

"The fact is I possessed a yacht of my own not so very long ago, and I captained her and I ran her engines on different occasions."

"That might be a recommendation, or it might not. If, as captain, you wrecked your vessel, or if, as engineer, you blew her up, these actions would hardly be a certificate of competency."

"I did neither. I sold the yacht in New York for what it would bring."

"How much money did you have when you bought your yacht?"

"I had what you would call half a million."

"Why do you say what I would call half a million? What would you call it?"

"I should call it a hundred thousand."

"Ah, I see. You're talking of pounds, and I'm talking of dollars. You're an Englishman, I suspect. Are you an educated man?"

"Moderately so. Eton and Oxford," said I, the champagne beginning to have its usual effect on a hungry man. However, the announcement of Eton and Oxford had no effect upon Mr. Hemster, so it did not matter.

"Come, young fellow," he said, with some impatience, "tell me all about yourself, and don't have to be drawn out like a witness on the stand."

"Very well," said I, "here is my story. After I left Oxford I had some little influence, as you might call it."

"No, a 'pull,' I would call it. All right, where did it land you?"

"It landed me as secretary to a Minister of the Crown."

"You don't mean a preacher?"

"No, I mean the Minister of Foreign Affairs, and he put me into the diplomatic service when he found the Government was going to be defeated. I was secretary of legation at Pekin and also here in Japan."

I filled myself another glass of champagne, and, holding it up to see the sparkles, continued jauntily:

"If I may go so far as to boast, I may say I was entrusted with several delicate missions, and I carried them through with reasonable success. I can both read and write the Japanese language, and I know a smattering of Chinese and a few dialects of the East, which have stood me in good stead more than once. To tell the truth, I was in a fair way for promotion and honor when unfortunately a relative died and left me the hundred thousand pounds that I spoke of."

"Why unfortunately? If you had had any brains you could have made that into millions."

"Yes, I suppose I could. I thought I was going to

17

do it. I bought myself a yacht at Southampton and sailed for New York. To make a long story short, it was a gold mine and a matter of ten weeks which were taken up with shooting and fishing in Canada. Then I had the gold mine and the experience, while the other fellow had the cash. He was good enough to pay me a trifle for my steam yacht, which, as the advertisements say, was 'of no further use to the owner.'"

As I sipped my champagne, the incidents I was relating seemed to recede farther and farther back and become of little consequence. In fact I felt like laughing over them, and although in sober moments I should have called the action of the man who got my money a swindle, under the influence of dry '78 his scheme became merely a very clever exercise of wit. Mr. Hemster was looking steadily at me, and for once his cigar was almost motionless.

"Well, well," he murmured, more to himself than to me, "I have always said the geographical position of New York gives it a tremendous advantage over Chicago. They never let the fools come West. They have always the first whack at the moneyed Englishman, and will have until we get a ship canal that will let the liners through to Chicago direct. Fleeced in ten weeks! Well, well! Go on, my son. What did you do after you 'd sold your yacht?"

"I took what money I had and made for the West."

"Came to Chicago?"

"Yes, I did."

"Just our luck. After you had been well buncoed

you came to Chicago. I swear I'm tempted to settle in New York when I get back."

"By the West I do not mean Chicago, Mr. Hemster. I went right through to San Francisco and took a steamer for Japan. I thought my knowledge of the East and of the languages might be of advantage. I was ashamed to return to England when I found I could make no headway here. I tried to bring influence to bear to get reinstated in the diplomatic service, but my brand of statesman was out of office and nothing could be done. I lived too expensively here at first, hoping to make an impression and gain a foothold that was worth having, and when I began to economize it was too late. I took to living in the native quarter, and descended from trying to get a clerkship into the position of a man who is willing to take anything. From my veranda on the hill up yonder I saw this boat come in, like a white-winged sea-gull, and so I came down, got into a sampan, and here I am, enjoying the best meal I've had for a long time. 'Here endeth the first lesson,'" I concluded irreverently, pouring out another glass of champagne.

Mr. Hemster did not reply for some moments. He was evidently ruminating, and the end of his cigar went round and round quicker and quicker.

"What might your name be?" he said at last.

"Rupert Tremorne."

"Got a handle to it?"

"A title? Oh, no! Plain Mr. Tremorne."

"I should say, off-hand, that a title runs in your family somewhere."

"Well; I admit that Lord Tremorne is my cousin, and we have a few others scattered about. However, there's little danger of it ever falling upon me. To tell the truth, the family for the last few years has no idea where I am, and now that I have lost my money I don't suppose they care very much. At least I have seen no advertisements in the papers, asking for a man of my description."

"If you were secretary to the Minister of whatever you call it, I don't know but what you'd do for me. I am short of a private secretary just at the present moment, and I think you'd do."

Whether it was the champagne, or the sandwiches, or the prospect of getting something to do, and consequently being able to pay my way, or all three combined, I felt like throwing my hat into the air and uttering a war-whoop; but something of native stolidity counterbalanced the effect of the stimulant, and I was astonished to hear myself reply very quietly:

"It would be folly for a man who had just applied for the position of stoker to pretend he is not elated at being offered a secretaryship. It is needless to say, Mr. Hemster, that I accept with alacrity and gratitude."

"Then that's settled," said the millionaire curtly. "As to the matter of salary, I think you would be wise to leave that to me. I have paid out a good deal of money recently and got mighty little for it. If you can turn the tide so that there is value received, you will find me liberal in the matter of wages."

"I am quite content to leave it so," I rejoined, "but

I think I ought in honesty to tell you, if you are expecting a shrewd business man as your secretary who will turn the tide of fortune in any way, you are likely to be disappointed in me. I am afraid I am a very poor business man."

"I am aware of that already," replied Hemster. "I can supply all the business qualifications that are needed in this new combination. What I want of you is something entirely different. You said you could speak more languages than your own?"

"Yes, I am very familiar with French and German, and have also a smattering of Spanish and Italian. I can read and write Japanese, speaking that language and Chinese with reasonable fluency, and can even jabber a little in Corean."

"Then you're my man," said my host firmly. "I suppose now you would not object to a little something on account?"

"I should be very much obliged indeed if you have confidence enough in me to make an advance. There are some things I should like to buy before I come aboard, and, not to put too fine a point to it, there are some debts I should like to settle."

"That's all right," commented Hemster shortly, thrusting his hand deep in his trousers pocket, and bringing out a handful of money which he threw on the wicker table. "There ought to be something like two hundred dollars there. Just count it and see, and write me a receipt for it."

I counted it, and, as I did so, thought he watched me rather keenly out of the corner of his eye. There was more than two hundred dollars in the heap, and I told him the amount. The Japanese brought up a sheet of paper headed with a gorgeous gilt and scarlet monogram and a picture of the yacht, and I wrote and signed the receipt.

"Do you know anything about the stores in town?" he asked, nodding his head toward Nagasaki.

"Oh, yes!"

"They tell me Nagasaki is a great place for buying crockery. I wish you would order sent to the yacht three complete dinner sets, three tea sets, and three luncheon sets. There is always a good deal of breakage on a sea-going yacht."

"Quite so," I replied. "Is there any particular pattern you wish, or any limit to the price?"

"Oh, I don't need expensive sets; anything will do. I'm not particular; in fact, I don't care even to see them; I leave that entirely to you, but tell the man to pack them securely, each in a separate box. He is to bring them aboard at half-past five this afternoon precisely, and ask for me. Now, when can you join us?"

"To-morrow morning, if that will be soon enough."

"Very well; to-morrow morning at ten."

I saw that he wished the interview terminated, as, for the last few minutes, he had exhibited signs of uneasiness. I therefore rose and said,— rather stammeringly, I am afraid:

"Mr. Hemster, I don't know how to thank you for your kindness in——"

"Oh, that's all right; that's all right," he replied

hastily, waving his hand; but before anything further could be spoken there came up on deck the most beautiful and stately creature I had ever beheld, superbly attired. She cast not even a glance at me, but hurried toward Mr. Hemster, crying impetuously:

"Oh, Poppa! I want to go into the town and shop!"

"Quite right, my dear," said the old man; "I wonder you've been so long about it. We've been in harbor two or three hours. This is Mr. Rupert Tremorne, my new private secretary. Mr. Tremorne, my daughter."

I made my bow, but it seemed to pass unnoticed.

"How do you do," said the girl hastily; then, to her father, "Poppa, I want some money!"

"Certainly, certainly, certainly," repeated the old gentleman, plunging his hand into his other pocket and pulling out another handful of the "necessary." As I learned afterward, each of his pockets seemed to be a sort of safe depository, which would turn forth any amount of capital when searched. He handed the accumulation to her, and she stuffed it hastily into a small satchel that hung at her side.

"You are going to take Miss Stretton with you?" he asked.

"Why, of course."

"Mr. Tremorne is cousin to Lord Tremorne, of England," said the old gentleman very slowly and solemnly.

I had been standing there rather stupidly, instead of taking my departure, as I should have done, for I may as well confess that I was astounded at the sumptuous beauty of the girl before me, who had hitherto cast not even a look in my direction. Now she raised her lovely, indescribable eyes to mine, and I felt a thrill extend to my finger-tips. Many handsome women have I seen in my day, but none to compare with this superb daughter of the West.

"Really!" she exclaimed with a most charming intonation of surprise. Then she extended a white and slim hand to me, and continued, "I am very glad to meet you, Mr. Tremorne. Do you live in Nagasaki?"

"I have done so for the past year."

"Then you know the town well?"

"I know it very well indeed."

At this juncture another young woman came on deck, and Miss Hemster turned quickly toward her.

"Oh, Hilda!" she cried, "I shall not need you to-day. Thanks ever so much."

"Not need her?" exclaimed her father. "Why, you can't go into Nagasaki alone, my dear."

"I have no intention of doing so," she replied amiably, "if Mr. Tremorne will be good enough to escort me."

"I shall be delighted," I gasped, expecting an expostulation from her father; but the old gentleman merely said:

"All right, my dear; just as you please."

"Rupert, my boy!" I said to my amazed self; "your ship has come in with a vengeance."

24

CHAPTER III

A STAIRWAY was slung on the other side of the yacht from that on which I had ascended, and at its foot lay a large and comfortable boat belonging to the yacht, manned by four stout seamen. Down this stairway and into the boat I escorted Miss Hemster. She seated herself in the stern and took the tiller-ropes in her hands, now daintily gloved. I sat down opposite to her and was about to give a command to the men to give way when she forestalled me, and the oars struck the water simultaneously. As soon as we had rounded the bow of the yacht there was a sudden outcry from a half-naked Japanese boy who was sculling about in a sampan.

"What's the matter with him?" asked Miss Hemster with a little laugh. "Does he think we're going to desert this boat and take that floating coffin of his?"

"I think it is my own man," I said; "and he fears that his fare is leaving him without settling up. Have I your permission to stop these men till he comes alongside? He has been waiting patiently for me while I talked with Mr. Hemster."

"Why, certainly," said the girl, and in obedience to her order the crew held water, and as the boy came alongside I handed him more than double what I owed him, and he nearly upset his craft by bowing in amazed acknowledgment.

"You're an Englishman, I suppose," said Miss Hemster.

"In a sort of way I am, but really a citizen of the world. For many years past I have been less in England than in other countries."

"For many years? Why, you talk as if you were an old man, and you don't look a day more than thirty."

"My looks do not libel me, Miss Hemster," I replied with a laugh, "for I am not yet thirty."

"I am twenty-one," she said carelessly, "but every one says I don't look more than seventeen."

"I thought you were younger than seventeen," said I, "when I first saw you a moment ago."

"Did you really? I think it is very flattering of you to say so, and I hope you mean it."

"I do, indeed, Miss Hemster."

"Do you think I look younger than Hilda?" she asked archly, "most people do."

"Hilda!" said I. "What Hilda?"

"Why, Hilda Stretton, my companion."

"I have never seen her."

"Oh, yes, you did; she was standing at the companion-way and was coming with me when I preferred to come with you."

"I did not see her," I said, shaking my head; "I saw no one but you."

The young lady laughed merrily,— a melodious ripple of sound. I have heard women's laughter compared to the tinkle of silver bells, but to that musical

tintinnabulation was now added something so deli-
ciously human and girlish that the whole effect was
nothing short of enchanting. Conversation now ceased,
for we were drawing close to the shore. I directed the
crew where to land, and the young lady sprang up the
steps without assistance from me,—before, indeed, I
could proffer any. I was about to follow when one
of the sailors touched me on the shoulder.

"The old man," he said in a husky whisper, nodding his head toward the yacht, "told me to tell you
that when you buy that crockery you're not to let Miss
Hemster know anything about it."

"Aren't you coming?" cried Miss Hemster to me
from the top of the wharf.

I ascended the steps with celerity and begged her
pardon for my delay.

"I am not sprightly seventeen, you see," I said.

She laughed, and I put her in a 'rickshaw drawn by
a stalwart Japanese, got into one myself, and we set
off for the main shopping street. I was rather at a
loss to know exactly what the sailor's message meant,
but I took it to be that for some reason Mr. Hemster
did not wish his daughter to learn that he was indulg-
ing so freely in dinner sets. As it was already three
o'clock in the afternoon, I realized that there would be
some difficulty in getting the goods aboard by five
o'clock, unless the young lady dismissed me when we
arrived at the shops. This, however, did not appear
to be her intention in the least; when our human steeds
stopped, she gave me her hand lightly as she
descended, and then said, with her captivating smile:

" I want you to take me at once to a china shop."

" To a what? " I cried.

" To a shop where they sell dishes,—dinner sets and that sort of thing. You know what I mean,— a crockery store."

I did, but I was so astonished by the request coming right on the heels of the message from her father, and taken in conjunction with his previous order, that I am afraid I stood looking very much like a fool, whereupon she laughed heartily, and I joined her. I saw she was quite a merry young lady, with a keen sense of the humour of things.

" Have n't they any crockery stores in this town? " she asked.

" Oh, there are plenty of them," I replied.

" Why, you look as if you had never heard of such a thing before. Take me, then, to whichever is the best. I want to buy a dinner set and a tea set the very first thing."

I bowed, and, somewhat to my embarrassment, she took my arm, tripping along by my side as if she were a little girl of ten, overjoyed at her outing, to which feeling she gave immediate expression.

" Is n't this jolly? " she cried.

" It is the most undeniably jolly shopping excursion I ever engaged in," said I, fervently and truthfully.

" You see," she went on, " the delight of this sort of thing is that we are in an utterly foreign country and can do just as we please. That is why I did not wish Hilda to come with us. She is rather prim and has notions of propriety which are all right at home, but what is the use of coming to foreign countries if you cannot enjoy them as you wish to?"

"I think that is a very sensible idea," said I.

"Why, it seems as if you and I were members of a travelling theatrical company, and were taking part in 'The Mikado,' does n't it? What funny little people they are all around us! Nagasaki does n't seem real. It looks as if it were set on a stage,—don't you think so?"

"Well, you know, I am rather accustomed to it. I have lived here for more than a year, as I told you."

"Oh, so you said. I have not got used to it yet. Have you ever seen 'The Mikado?'"

"Do you mean the Emperor or the play?"

"At the moment I was thinking of the play."

"Yes, I have seen it, and the real Mikado, too, and spoken with him."

"Have you, indeed? How lucky you are!"

"You speak truly, Miss Hemster, and I never knew how lucky I was until to-day."

She bent her head and laughed quietly to herself. I thought we were more like a couple of school children than members of a theatrical troupe, but as I never was an actor I cannot say how the latter behave when they are on the streets of a strange town.

"Oh, I have met your kind of man before, Mr. Tremorne. You don't mind what you say when you are talking to a lady as long as it is something flattering."

"I assure you, Miss Hemster, that quite the con-

trary is the case. I never flatter; and if I have been
using a congratulatory tone it has been directed entirely
to myself and to my own good fortune."

"There you go again. How did you come to meet
the Mikado?"

"I used to be in the diplomatic service in Japan, and
my duties on several occasions brought me the honor
of an audience with His Majesty."

"How charmingly you say that, and I can see that
you believe it from your heart; and although we are
democratic, I believe it, too. I always love diplomatic
society, and enjoyed a good deal of it in Washington,
and my imagination always pictured behind them the
majesty of royalty, so I have come abroad to see the
real thing. I was presented at Court in London, Mr.
Tremorne. Now, please don't say that you congratulate the Court!"

"There is no need of my saying it, as it has already
been said; or perhaps I should say 'it goes without
saying.'"

"Thank you very much, Mr. Tremorne; I think
you are the most polite man I ever met. I want you
to do me a very great favor and introduce me to the
higher grades of diplomatic society in Nagasaki during
our stay here."

"I regret, Miss Hemster, that that is impossible,
because I have been out of the service for some years
now. Besides, the society here is consular rather than
diplomatic. The Legation is at the capital, you know.
Nagasaki is merely a commercial city."

"Oh, is it? I thought perhaps you had been seeing

my father to-day because of some consular business, or that sort of thing, pertaining to the yacht."

As the girl said this I realized, with a suddenness that was disconcerting, the fact that I was practically acting under false pretences. I was her father's humble employee, and she did not know it. I remembered with a pang when her father first mentioned my name she paid not the slightest attention to it; but when he said I was the cousin of Lord Tremorne the young lady had favored me with a glance I was not soon to forget. Therefore, seeing that Mr. Hemster had neglected to make my position clear, it now became my duty to give some necessary explanation, so that his daughter might not continue an acquaintance that was rapidly growing almost intimate under her misapprehension as to who I was. I saw with a pang that a humiliation was in store for me such as always lies in wait for a man who momentarily steps out of his place and receives consideration which is not his social due.

I had once before suffered the experience which was now ahead of me, and it was an episode I did not care to repeat, although I failed to see how it could be honestly avoided. On my return to Japan I sought out the man in the diplomatic service who had been my greatest friend and for whom I had in former days accomplished some slight services, because my status in the ranks was superior to his own. Now that there was an opportunity for a return of these services, I called upon him, and was received with a cordiality that went to my discouraged heart; but the moment he learned

I was in need, and that I could not regain the place I
had formerly held, he congealed in the most tactful
manner possible. It was an interesting study in human
deportment. His manner and words were simply un-
impeachable, but there gathered around him a mantle
of impenetrable frigidity the collection of which was a
triumph in tactful intercourse. As he grew colder and
colder, I grew hotter and hotter. I managed to withdraw without showing, I hope, the deep humiliation I
felt. Since that time I had never sought a former acquaintance, or indeed any countryman of my own, preferring to be indebted to my old friend Yansan on the
terrace above or the sampan-boy on the waters below.
The man I speak of has risen high and is rising higher
in my old profession, and every now and then his last
words ring in my ears and warm them,—words of
counterfeit cordiality as he realized they were the last
that he should probably ever speak to me:

"Well, my dear fellow, I'm ever so glad you called.
If I can do anything for you, you must be sure and
let me know."

As I had already let him know, my reply that I
should certainly do so must have sounded as hollow as
his own smooth phrase.

Unpleasant as that episode was, the situation was
now ten times worse, as it involved a woman,—and a
lovely woman at that,—who had treated me with a
kindness she would feel misplaced when she understood the truth. However, there was no help for it,
so, clearing my throat, I began:

"Miss Hemster, when I took the liberty of calling

32

on your father this morning, I was a man penniless and out of work. I went to the yacht in the hope that I might find something to do. I was fortunate enough to be offered the position of private secretary to Mr. Hemster, which position I have accepted."

The young lady, as I expected, instantly withdrew her hand from my arm, and stood there facing me, I also coming to a halt; and thus we confronted each other in the crowded street of Nagasaki. Undeniable amazement overspread her beautiful countenance.

" Why! " she gasped, " you are, then, Poppa's hired man ? "

I winced a trifle, but bowed low to her.

" Madam," I replied, " you have stated the fact with great truth and terseness."

" Do you mean to say," she said, " that you are to be with us after this on the yacht ? "

" I suspect such to be your father's intention." Then, to my amazement, she impulsively thrust forth both her hands and clasped mine.

" Why, how perfectly lovely! " she exclaimed. " I have n't had a white man to talk with except Poppa for ages and ages. But you must remember that everything I want you to do, you are to do. You are to be *my* hired man; Poppa won't mind."

" You will find me a most devoted retainer, Miss Hemster."

" I do love that word 'retainer,'" she cried enthusiastically. " It is like the magic talisman of the 'Arabian Nights,' and conjures up at once visions of a historic tower, mullioned windows, and all that sort of thing. When you were made a bankrupt, Mr. Tremorne, was there one faithful old retainer who refused to desert you as the others had done?"

"Ah, my dear young lady, you are thinking of the romantic drama now, as you were alluding to comic opera a little while ago. I believe, in the romantic drama, the retainer, like the man with the mortgage, never lets go. I am thankful to say I had no such person in my employ. He would have been an awful nuisance. It was hard enough to provide for myself, not to mention a retainer. But here we are at the crockery shop."

I escorted her in, and she was soon deeply absorbed in the mysteries of this pattern or that of the various wares exposed to her choice. Meanwhile I took the opportunity to give the proprietor instructions in his own language to send to the yacht before five o'clock what Mr. Hemster had ordered, and I warned the man he was not to mix up the order I had just given him with that of the young lady. The Japanese are very quick at comprehension, and when Miss Hemster and I left the place I had no fear of any complication arising through my instructions.

We wandered from shop to shop, the girl enthusiastic over Nagasaki, much to my wonder, for there are other places in Japan more attractive than this commercial town; but the glamor of the East cast its spell over the young woman, and, although I was rather tired of the Orient, I must admit that the infection of her high spirits extended to my own feelings. A week ago it would have appeared impossible that I should be enjoying myself so thoroughly as I was now doing. It seemed as if years had rolled from my shoulders, and I was a boy once more, living in a world where conventionality was unknown.

The girl herself was in a whirlwind of glee, and it was not often that the shopkeepers of Nagasaki met so easy a victim. She seemed absolutely reckless in the use of money, paying whatever was asked for anything that took her fancy. In a very short time all her ready cash was gone, but that made not the slightest difference. She ordered here and there with the extravagance of a queen, on what she called the " C. O. D." plan, which I afterward learned was an American phrase meaning, " Collect on delivery." Her peregrinations would have tired out half-a-dozen men, but she showed no signs of fatigue. I felt a hesitation about inviting her to partake of refreshment, but I need not have been so backward.

" Talking of comic operas," she exclaimed as we came out of the last place, " Are n't there any teahouses here, such as we see on the stage? "

" Yes, plenty of them," I replied.

" Well," she exclaimed with a ripple of laughter, " take me to the wickedest of them. What is the use of going around the world in a big yacht if you don't see life? "

I wondered what her father would say if he knew, but I acted the faithful retainer to the last, and did as I was bid. She expressed the utmost delight in everything she saw, and it was well after six o'clock when we descended from our 'rickshaw at the landing. The boat was awaiting us, and in a short time we were alongside the yacht once more. It had been a wild, tempestuous outing, and I somewhat feared the stern disapproval of an angry parent. He was leaning over the rail revolving an unlit cigar.

"Oh, Poppa!" she cried up at him with enthusiasm, "I have had a perfectly splendid time. Mr. Tremorne knows Nagasaki like a book. He has taken me everywhere," she cried, with unnecessary emphasis on the last word.

The millionaire was entirely unperturbed.

"That's all right," he said. "I hope you haven't tired yourself out."

"Oh, no! I should be delighted to do it all over again! Has anybody sent anything aboard for me?"

"Yes," said the old man, "there's been a procession of people here since you left. Dinner's ready, Mr. Tremorne. You'll come aboard, of course, and take pot-luck with us?"

"No, thank you, Mr. Hemster," I said; "I must get a sampan and make my way into town again."

"Just as you say; but you don't need a sampan, these men will row you back again. See you to-morrow at ten, then."

Miss Hemster, now on deck, leaned over the rail and daintily blew me a kiss from the tips of her slender fingers.

"Thank you so much, retainer," she cried, as I lifted my hat in token of farewell.

CHAPTER IV

I WAS speedily rowed ashore in a state of great exaltation. The sudden change in my expectations was bewilderingly Eastern in its completeness. The astonishingly intimate companionship of this buoyant, effervescent girl had affected me as did the bottle of champagne earlier in the day. I was well aware that many of my former acquaintances would have raised their hands in horror at the thought of a girl wandering about an Eastern city with me, entirely unchaperoned; but I had been so long down on my luck, and the experiences I had encountered with so-called fashionable friends had been so bitter, that the little finicky rules of society seemed of small account when compared with the realities of life. The girl was perfectly untrained and impulsive, but that she was a true-hearted woman I had not the slightest doubt. Was I in love with her? I asked myself, and at that moment my brain was in too great a whirl to be able to answer the question satisfactorily to myself. My short ten weeks in America had given me no such acquaintance as this, although the two months and a half had cost me fifty thousand dollars a week, certainly the most expensive living that any man is likely to encounter. I had met a few American women, but they

37

all seemed as cold and indifferent as our own, while
here was a veritable child of nature, as untrammelled
by the little rules of society as could well be imagined.
After all, were these rules so important as I had hitherto supposed them to be? Certainly not, I replied to
myself, as I stepped ashore.

I climbed the steep hill to my former residence with
my head in the air in every sense of the word. Many
a weary journey I had taken up that forlorn path, and
it had often been the up-hill road of discouragement;
but to-night Japan was indeed the land of enchantment
which so many romantic writers have depicted it. I
thought of the girl and thought of her father, wondering what my new duties were to be. If to-day were a
sample of them then truly was Paradise regained, as
the poet has it. I had told Mr. Hemster that I needed
time to purchase necessary things for the voyage, but
this would take me to very few shops. I had in store
in Nagasaki a large trunk filled with various suits of
clothing, a trunk of that comprehensive kind which
one buys in America. This was really in pawn. I had
delivered it to a shopkeeper who had given me a line of
credit now long since ended, but I knew I should find
my goods and chattels safe when I came with the
money, as indeed proved to be the case.

It was a great pleasure to meet Yansan once more,
bowing as lowly as if I were in truth a millionaire. I
had often wondered what would happen if I had been
compelled to tell the grimacing old fellow I had no
money to pay him. Would his excessive politeness
have stood the strain? Perhaps so, but luckily his

good nature was not to be put to the test. I could scarcely refrain from grasping his two hands, as Miss Hemster had grasped mine, and dancing with him around the bare habitation which he owned and which had so long been my shelter. However, I said calmly to him:

"Yansan, my ship has come in, as I told you this morning; and now, if you will bring me that bill, errors and all, I will pay you three times its amount."

Speechless, the old man dropped on his knees and beat his forehead against the floor.

"Excellency has always been too good to me!" he exclaimed.

I tried to induce good old Yansan to share supper with me; but he was too much impressed with my greatness and could do nothing but bow and bow and serve me.

After the repast I went down into the town again, redeemed my trunk and its contents, bought what I needed, and ordered everything forwarded to the yacht before seven o'clock next morning. Then I went to a tea-house, and drank tea, and thought over the wonderful events of the day, after which I climbed the hill again for a night's rest.

I was very sorry to bid farewell to old Yansan next morning, and I believe he was very sorry to part with his lodger. Once more at the waterside I hailed my sampan-boy, who was now all eagerness to serve me, and he took me out to the yacht, which was evidently ready for an early departure. Her whole crew was now aboard, and most of them had had a day's leave in

Nagasaki yesterday. The captain was pacing up and down the bridge, and smoke was lazily trailing from the funnel.

Arrived on deck I found Mr. Hemster in his former position in the cane chair, with his back still toward Nagasaki, which town I believe he never glanced at all the time his yacht was in harbor. I learned afterward that he thought it compared very unfavorably with Chicago. His unlighted cigar was describing circles in the air, and all in all I might have imagined he had not changed from the position I left him in the day before if I had not seen him leaning over the rail when I escorted his daughter back to the yacht. He gave me no further greeting than a nod, which did not err on the side of effusiveness.

I inquired of the Japanese boy, who stood ready to receive me with all the courtesy of his race, whether my luggage had come aboard, and he informed me that it had. I approached Mr. Hemster, bidding him good-morning, but he gave a side nod of his head toward the Japanese boy and said, " He 'll show you to your cabin," so I followed the youth down the companion-way to my quarters. The yacht, as I have said, was very big. The main saloon extended from side to side, and was nearly as large as the dining-room of an ocean liner. Two servants with caps and aprons, exactly like English housemaids, were dusting and putting things to rights as I passed through.

My cabin proved ample in size, and was even more comfortably equipped than I expected to find it. My luggage was there, and I took the opportunity of changing my present costume for one of more nautical cut, and, placing a yachting-cap on my head, I went on deck again. I had expected, from all the preparedness I had seen, to hear the anchor-chain rattle up before I was equipped, and feared for the moment that I had delayed the sailing of the yacht; but on looking at my watch as I went on deck I found it was not yet ten o'clock, so I was in ample time, as had been arranged.

I had seen nothing of Miss Hemster, and began to suspect that she had gone ashore and that the yacht was awaiting her return; but a glance showed me that all the yacht's boats were in place, so if the young woman had indulged in a supplementary shopping-tour it must have been in a sampan, which was unlikely.

The old gentleman, as I approached him, eyed my yachting toggery with what seemed to me critical disapproval.

" Well," he said, " you 're all fitted out for a cruise, are n't you? Have a cigar,"—and he offered me his case.

I took the weed and replied:

" Yes, and you seem ready to begin a cruise. May I ask where you are going? "

" I don't know exactly," he replied carelessly. " I have n't quite made up my mind yet. I thought perhaps you might be able to decide the matter."

" To decide! " I answered in surprise.

" Yes," he said, sitting up suddenly and throwing the cigar overboard. " What nonsense were you talking to my daughter yesterday? "

I was so taken aback at this unexpected and gruff inquiry that I fear I stood there looking rather idiotic, which was evidently the old man's own impression of me, for he scowled in a manner that was extremely disconcerting. I had no wish to adopt the Adam-like expedient of blaming the woman; but, after all, he had been there when I went off alone with her, and it was really not my fault that I was the girl's sole companion in Nagasaki. All my own early training and later social prejudices led me to sympathize with Mr. Hemster's evident ill-humour regarding our shore excursion, but nevertheless it struck me as a trifle belated. He should have objected when the proposal was made.

"Really, sir," I stammered at last, "I'm afraid I must say I don't exactly know what you mean."

"I think I spoke plainly enough," he answered. "I want you to be careful what you say, and if you come with me to my office, where we shall not be interrupted, I'll give you a straight talking to, so that we may avoid trouble in the future."

I was speechless with amazement, and also somewhat indignant. If he took this tone with me, my place was evidently going to be one of some difficulty. However, needs must when the devil drives, even if he comes from Chicago; and although his words were bitter to endure, I was in a manner helpless and forced to remember my subordinate position, which, in truth, I had perhaps forgotten during my shopping experiences with his impulsive daughter. Yet I had myself made her aware of my situation, and if our conversation at times had been a trifle free and easy I think the fault —— but there — there — there —— I'm at the Adam business again. The woman tempted me, and I did talk. I felt humiliated that even to myself I placed any blame upon her.

Mr. Hemster rose, nipped off the point of another cigar, and strode along the deck to the companion-way, I following him like a confessed culprit. He led me to what he called his office, a room not very much larger than my own, but without the bunk that took up part of the space in my cabin; in fact a door led out of it which, I afterward learned, communicated with his bedroom. The office was fitted up with an American roll-top desk fastened to the floor, a copying-press, a typewriter, filing-cases from floor to ceiling, and other paraphernalia of a completely equipped business establishment. There was a swivelled armchair before the desk, into which Mr. Hemster dropped and leaned back, the springs creaking as he did so. There was but one other chair in the room, and he motioned me into it.

"See here!" he began abruptly. "Did you tell my daughter yesterday that you were a friend of the Mikado's?"

"God bless me, no!" I was surprised into replying. "I said nothing of the sort."

"Well, you left her under that impression."

"I cannot see, Mr. Hemster, how such can be the case. I told Miss Hemster that I had met the Mikado on several occasions, but I explained to her that these occasions were entirely official, and each time I merely accompanied a superior officer in the diplomatic service. Although I have spoken with His Majesty, it was merely because questions were addressed to me, and because I was the only person present sufficiently conversant with the Japanese language to make him a reply in his own tongue."

" I see, I see," mused the old gentleman; "but Gertie somehow got it into her head that you could introduce us personally to the Mikado. I told her it was not likely that a fellow I had picked up strapped from the streets of Nagasaki, as one might say, would be able to give us an introduction that would amount to anything."

I felt myself getting red behind the ears as Mr. Hemster put my situation with, what seemed to me, such unnecessary brutality. Yet, after all, what he had said was the exact truth, and I had no right to complain of it, for if there was money in my pocket at that moment it was because he had placed it there; and then I saw intuitively that he meant no offence, but was merely repeating what he had said to his daughter, placing the case in a way that would be convincing to a man, whatever effect it might have on a woman's mind.

" I am afraid," I said, " that I must have expressed myself clumsily to Miss Hemster. I think I told her,— but I make the statement subject to correction,—that I had so long since severed my connection with diplomatic service in Tokio that even the slight power I then possessed no longer exists. If I still retained my former position I should scarcely be more helpless than I am now, so far as what you require is concerned."

44

"That's exactly what I told her," growled the old man. "I suppose you haven't any suggestion to make that would help me out at all?"

"The only suggestion I can make is this, and indeed I think the way seems perfectly clear. You no doubt know your own Ambassador,— perhaps have letters of introduction to him,— and he may very easily arrange for you to have an audience with His Majesty the Mikado."

"Oh! our Ambassador!" growled Mr. Hemster in tones of great contempt; "he's nothing but a one-horse politician."

"Nevertheless," said I, "his position is such that by merely exercising the prerogatives of his office he could get you what you wanted."

"No, he can't," maintained the old gentleman stoutly. "Still, I shouldn't say anything against him; he's all right. He did his best for us, and if we could have waited long enough at Yokohama perhaps he might have fixed up an audience with the Mikado. But I'd had enough of hanging on around there, and so I sailed away. Now, my son, I said I was going to give you a talking to, and I am. I'll tell you just how the land lies, so you can be of some help to me and not a drawback. I want you to be careful of what you say to Gertie about such people as the Mikado, because it excites her and makes her think certain things are easy when they're not."

"I am very sorry if I have said anything that led to a misapprehension. I certainly did not intend to."

"No, no! I understand that. I am not blaming you

45

a bit. I just want you to catch on to the situation, that's all. Gertie likes you first rate; she told me so, and I'm ever so much obliged to you for the trouble you took yesterday afternoon in entertaining her. She told me everything you said and did, and it was all right. Now Gertie has always been accustomed to moving in the very highest society. She does n't care for anything else, and she took to you from the very first. I was glad of that, because I should have consulted her before I hired you. Nevertheless, I knew the moment you spoke that you were the man I wanted, and so I took the risk. I never cared for high society myself; my intercourse has been with business men. I understand them, and I like them; but I don't cut any figure in high society, and I don't care to, either. Now, with Gertie it's different. She's been educated at the finest schools, and I've taken her all over Europe, where we stayed at the very best hotels and met the very best people in both Europe and America. Why, we've met more Sirs and Lords and Barons and High Mightinesses than you can shake a stick at. Gertie, she's right at home among those kind of people, and, if I do say it myself, she's quite capable of taking her place among the best of them, and she knows it. There never was a time we came in to the best table d'hôte in Europe that every eye was n't turned toward her, and she's been the life of the most noted hotels that exist, no matter where they are, and no matter what their price is."

I ventured to remark that I could well believe this to have been the case.

A CHICAGO PRINCESS

"Yes, and you don't need to take my word for it," continued the old man with quite perceptible pride; "you may ask any one that was there. Whether it was a British Lord, or a French Count, or a German Baron, or an Italian Prince, it was just the same. I admit that it seemed to me that some of those nobles did n't amount to much. But that's neither here nor there; as I told you before, I'm no judge. I suppose they have their usefulness in creation, even though I'm not able to see it. But the result of it all was that Gertie got tired of them, and, as she is an ambitious girl and a real lady, she determined to strike higher, and so, when we bought this yacht and came abroad again, she determined to go in for Kings, so I've been on a King hunt ever since, and to tell the truth it has cost me a lot of money and I don't like it. Not that I mind the money if it resulted in anything, but it has n't resulted in anything; that is, it has n't amounted to much. Gertie does n't care for the ordinary presentation at Court, for nearly anybody can have that. What she wants is to get a King or an Emperor right here on board this yacht at lunch or tea, or whatever he wants, and enjoy an intimate conversation with him, just like she's had with them no-account Princes. Then she wants a column or two account of that written up for the Paris edition of the "New York Herald," and she wants to have it cabled over to America. Now she's the only chick or child I've got. Her mother's been dead these fifteen years, and Gertie is all I have in the world, so I'm willing to do anything she wants done, no matter whether I like it or not. But I don't want to engage in anything that does n't succeed. Success is the one thing that amounts to anything. The man who is a failure cuts no ice. And so it rather grinds me to confess that I 've been a failure in this King business. Now I don't know much about Kings, but it strikes me they 're just like other things in this world. If you want to get along with them, you must study them. It 's like climbing a stair; if you want to get to the top you must begin at the lowest step. If you try to take one stride up to the top landing, why you 're apt to come down on your head. I told Gertie it was no use beginning with the German Emperor, for we 'd have to get accustomed to the low-down Kings and gradually work up. She believes in aiming high. That 's all right ordinarily, but it is n't a practical proposition. Still, I let her have her way and did the best I could, but it was no use. I paid a German Baron a certain sum for getting the Emperor on board my yacht, but he did n't deliver the goods. So I said to Gertie: ' My girl, we 'd better go to India, or some place where Kings are cheap, and practise on them first.' She hated to give in, but she 's a reasonable young woman if you take her the right way. Well, the long and the short of it was that we sent the yacht around to Marseilles, and went down from Paris to meet her there, and sailed to Egypt, and, just as I said, we had no difficulty at all in raking in the Khedive. But that was n't very satisfactory when all 's said and done. Gertie claimed he was n't a real king, and I say he 's not a real gentleman. We had a little unpleasantness there, and he became altogether too friendly, so we sailed off down through the Canal a hunting Kings, till at last we got here to Japan. Now we 're up against it once more, and I suppose this here Mikado has hobnobbed so much with real Emperors and that sort of thing that he thinks himself a white man like the rest. So I says to Gertie, ' There 's a genuine Emperor in Corea, good enough to begin on, and we 'll go there,' and that 's how we came round from Yokohama to Nagasaki, and dropped in here to get a few things we might not be able to obtain in Corea. The moment I saw you and learned that you knew a good deal about the East, it struck me that if I took you on as private secretary you would be able to give me a few points, and perhaps take charge of this business altogether. Do you think you 'd be able to do that?"

"Well," I said hesitatingly, "I 'm not sure, but if I can be of any use to you on such a quest it will be in Corea. I 've been there on two or three occasions, and each time had an audience with the King."

"Why do you call him the King? Is n't he an Emperor?"

"Well, I 've always called him the King, but I 've heard people term him the Emperor."

"The American papers always call him an Emperor. So you think you could manage it, eh?"

"I don't know that there would be any difficulty about the matter. Of course you are aware he is merely a savage."

"Well, they 're all savages out here, are n't they? I don't suppose he 's any worse or any better than the Mikado."

" Oh, the Mikado belongs to one of the most ancient civilizations in the world. I don't think the two potentates are at all on a par."

" Well, that's all right. That just bears out what I was saying, that it's the correct thing to begin with the lowest of them. You see I hate to admit I'm too old to learn anything, and I think I can learn this King business if I stick long enough at it. But I don't believe in a man trying to make a grand piano before he knows how to handle a saw. So you see, Mr. Tremorne, the position is just this. I want to sail for Corea, and Gertie, she wants to go back to Yokohama and tackle the Mikado again, thinking you can pull it off this time."

" I dislike very much to disagree with a lady," I said, " but I think your plan is the more feasible of the two. I do not think it would be possible to get the Mikado to come aboard this yacht, but it might be that the King of Corea would accept your invitation."

" What's the name of the capital of that place? " asked Mr. Hemster.

" It is spelled S-e-o-u-l, and is pronounced ' Sool.' "

" How far is it from here? "

" I don't know exactly, but it must be something like four hundred miles, perhaps a little more."

" It is on the sea? "

" No. It lies some twenty-six miles inland by road, and more than double that distance by the winding river Han."

" Can I steam up that river with this yacht to the capital? "

"No, I don't think you could. You could go part way, perhaps, but I imagine your better plan would be to moor at the port of Chemulpo and go to Seoul by road, although the road is none of the best."

"I've got a little naphtha launch on board. I suppose the river is big enough for us to go up to the capital in that?"

"Yes, I suppose you could do it in a small launch, but the river is so crooked that I doubt if you would gain much time, although you might gain in comfort."

"Very well, we'll make for that port, whatever you call it," said Hemster, rising. "Now, if you'll just take an armchair on deck, and smoke, I'll give instructions to the captain."

CHAPTER V

WE had been a long time together in the little
office, longer even than this extended conversation would lead a reader to imagine,
and as I went through the saloon I saw that they were
laying the table for lunch, a sight by no means ungrate-
ful to me, for I had risen early and enjoyed but a small
and frugal breakfast. I surmised from the prepara-
tions going forward that I should in the near future
have something better than rice. When I reached the
deck I saw the captain smoking a pipe and still pacing
the bridge with his hands in his pockets. He was a
grizzled old sea-dog, who, I found later, had come from
the Cape Cod district, and was what he looked, a most
capable man. I went aft and sat down, not wishing to
go forward and became acquainted with the captain,
as I expected every moment that Mr. Hemster would
come up and give him his sailing-orders. But time
passed on and nothing happened, merely the same state
of tension that occurs when every one is ready to move
and no move is made. At last the gong sounded for
lunch. I saw the captain pause in his promenade,
knock the ashes out of his pipe into the palm of his
hand, and prepare to go down. So I rose and descended the stairway, giving a nod of recognition to
the captain, who followed at my heels. The table was

laid for five persons. Mr. Hemster occupied the position at the head of it, and on his right sat his daughter, her head bent down over the tablecloth. On the opposite side, at Mr. Hemster's left, sat the young lady of whom I had had a glimpse the afternoon before. The captain pushed past me with a gruff, "How de do, all," which was not responded to. He took the place at the farther end of the table. If I have described the situation on deck as a state of tension, much more so was the atmosphere of the dining-saloon. The silence was painful, and, not knowing what better to do, I approached Miss Hemster and said pleasantly:

"Good-morning. I hope you are none the worse for your shopping expedition of yesterday."

The young woman did not look up or reply till her father said in beseeching tones:

"Gertie, Mr. Tremorne is speaking to you."

Then she glanced at me with eyes that seemed to sparkle dangerously.

"Oh, how do you do?" she said rapidly. "Your place is over there by Miss Stretton."

There was something so insulting in the tone and inflection that it made the words, simple as they were, seem like a slap in the face. Their purport seemed to be to put me in my proper position in that society, to warn me that, if I had been treated as a friend the day before, conditions were now changed, and I was merely, as she had previously remarked, her father's hired man. My situation was anything but an enviable one, and as there was nothing to say I merely bowed low to the girl, walked around behind the captain, and took

53

my place beside Miss Stretton, as I had been commanded to do. I confess I was deeply hurt by the studied insolence of look and voice; but a moment later I felt that I was probably making a mountain of a molehill, for the good, bluff captain said, as if nothing unusual had happened:

" That 's right, young man; I see you have been correctly brought up. Always do what the women tell you. Obey orders if you break owners. That 's what we do in our country. In our country, sir, we allow the women to rule, and their word is law, even though the men vote."

" Such is not the case in the East," I could not help replying.

" Why," said the captain, " it 's the East I 'm talking about. All throughout the Eastern States, yes, and the Western States, too."

" Oh, I beg your pardon," I replied, " I was referring to the East of Asia. The women don't rule in these countries."

" Well," said the staunch captain, " then that 's the reason they amount to so little. I never knew an Eastern country yet that was worth the powder to blow it up."

" I 'm afraid," said I, " that your rule does not prove universally good. It 's a woman who reigns in China, and I should n't hold that Empire up as an example to others."

The captain laughed heartily.

" Young man, you 're contradicting yourself. You 're excited, I guess. You said a minute ago that

54

women did n't rule in the East, and now you show that the largest country in the East *is* ruled by a woman. You can't have it both ways, you know."

I laughed somewhat dismally in sympathy with him, and, lunch now being served, the good man devoted his entire attention to eating. As no one else said a word except the captain and myself, I made a feeble but futile attempt to cause the conversation to become general. I glanced at my fair neighbor to the right, who had not looked up once since I entered. Miss Stretton was not nearly so handsome a girl as Miss Hemster, yet nevertheless in any ordinary company she would be regarded as very good-looking. She had a sweet and sympathetic face, and at the present moment it was rosy red.

"Have you been in Nagasaki?" I asked, which was a stupid question, for I knew she had not visited the town the day before, and unless she had gone very early there was no time for her to have been ashore before I came aboard.

She answered "No" in such low tones that, fearing I had not heard it, she cleared her throat, and said "No" again. Then she raised her eyes for one brief second, cast a sidelong glance at me, so appealing and so vivid with intelligence, that I read it at once to mean, "Oh, please do not talk to me."

The meal was most excellent, yet I never remember to have endured a half-hour so unpleasant. Across the table from me, Miss Hemster had pushed away plate after plate and had touched nothing. When I spoke to her companion she began drumming nervously

55

on the tablecloth with her fingers, as if she had great difficulty in preventing herself giving expression to an anger that was only too palpable. Her father went on stolidly with his lunch, and made no effort to relieve the rigor of the amazing situation. As soon as the main dish had been served and disposed of, the captain rose, and, nodding to the company, made for the companion-way. Once there he turned on his heel and said:

"Mr. Hemster, any orders?"

Before her father could reply, the young lady rose with an action so sudden and a gesture of her right hand so sweeping that the plate before her toppled and fell with a crash to the floor. I noticed Mr. Hemster instinctively grasp the tablecloth, but the girl marched away as erect as a grenadier, her shapely shoulders squared as if she was on military parade, and thus she disappeared into the forward part of the ship. Miss Stretton looked up at her employer, received a slight nod, then she, with a murmur of excuse to me, rose and followed the mistress of the ship. I heard a loud, angry voice, shrill as that of a peacock, for a moment, then a door was closed, and all was still. Mr. Hemster said slowly to the captain:

"I'll be up there in a minute and let you know where we're going. We've got all the time there is, you know."

"Certainly, sir," said the captain, disappearing.

There was nothing to say, so I said nothing, and Mr. Hemster and I sat out our lonely meal together. He seemed in no way perturbed by what had taken place, and as, after all, it was no affair of mine, even if my unfortunate remark regarding the Mikado had been the cause of it, I said inwardly there was little reason for my disturbing myself about it. Although the old gentleman showed no outward sign of inward commotion, he nevertheless seemed anxious that our dismal meal should draw to a speedy close, for he said to me at last:

"If you wish for coffee, you can have it served to you on deck."

"Thank you," said I, glad to avail myself of the opportunity to escape. As I mounted the companion-way I heard him say in firmer tones than I had known him to use before:

"Tell my daughter to come here to me,"— a command answered by the gentle "Yes, sir," of the Japanese boy.

I moved the wicker chair and table as far aft as possible, to be out of earshot should any remarks follow me from the saloon. I saw the captain on the bridge again, pacing up and down, pipe in mouth and hands in pockets. Even at that distance I noticed on his face a semi-comical grimace, and it actually seemed to me that he winked his left eye in my direction. The coffee did not come, and as I rose to stroll forward and converse with the captain I could not help hearing the low determined tones of the man down in the saloon, mingled now and then with the high-pitched, angry voice of the woman. As I hurried forward there next came up the companion-way a scream so terrible and ear-piercing that it must have startled every one on board, yet nobody moved. This was followed instantly by a crash, as if the table had been flung over, which of course was impossible, as it was fastened to the floor. Then came the hysterical, terrifying half-scream, half-sob of a woman apparently in mortal agony, and instinctively I started down the companion-way, to be met by Miss Stretton, who stretched her arms from side to side of the stairway. The appealing look I had noticed before was in her eyes, and she said in a low voice:

"Please don't come down. You can do no good."

"Is anybody hurt?" I cried.

"No, nobody, nobody. Please don't come down."

I turned back, and not wishing to see the captain or any one else at that moment, sat down in my chair again. The sobs died away, and then Mr. Hemster came up the companion-way with a determined look on his face which seemed to me to say, "Women do not rule after all." Once on deck he shouted out to the captain the one word:

"Corea!"

CHAPTER VI

THE shouting of those three syllables was like the utterance of a talismanic word in an Arabian legend. It cleft the spell of inactivity which hung over officers and crew as the sweep of a scimitar cuts through the web of enchantment. The silence was immediately broken by the agitated snorting of a pony-engine, and the rattle of the anchor-chain coming up. Then the melodious jingling of bells down below told the engineer to " stand by." As the snort of the engine and the rattle of the chain ceased, the crew mustered forward and began to stow the anchor. Another jingle below, and then began the pulsating of the engines, while the sharp prow of the yacht seemed slowly to brush aside the distant hills and set them moving. To a seasoned traveller like myself there is something stimulating in the first throb of an engine aboard ship. It means new scenes and fresh experiences. Farewell Nagasaki and starvation; yes, and sometimes despair. Yet I had a warm corner in my heart for the old commercial city, with its queer little picturesque inhabitants, whose keen eye for business was nevertheless frequently softened by sentiment.

The man whose sharply uttered words had called up commotion out of the stillness sank somewhat listlessly into his customary armchair, and put his feet, crossed, on the rail. There was something in his attitude that warned me he did not wish his privacy intruded upon, so I leaned over the opposite rail and steadfastly regarded the receding city. The big yacht moved smoothly and swiftly over the waters of Nagasaki Bay, which at that moment glittered dazzlingly in the sunlight. The craft was evidently well engined, for the vibration was scarcely perceptible, and somehow it gave one the consciousness that there was a reserve of power which might be called upon in a pinch. Once clear of Nagasaki Bay the captain laid her course due west, as if we were to race the declining sun. I surmised that a safe rather than a quick voyage was his object, and that he intended to strike through the Yellow Sea and avoid threading the mazes of the Corean Archipelago.

Long before the gong sounded for dinner we were out of sight of land. As I went down the companion stairs I must admit that I looked forward to the meal with some degree of apprehension, hoping the atmosphere would be less electric than during luncheon. I need have harboured no fear; Mr. Hemster, the captain, and myself sat down, but the ladies did not appear during the meal. Mr. Hemster had little to say, but the jovial captain told some excellent stories, which to his amazement and delight I laughed at, for he had a theory that no Englishman could see the point of any yarn that ever was spun. Mr. Hemster never once smiled; probably he had heard the stories before, and in the middle of dinner (such seemed to be the captain's impolite habit) the story-teller rose and left us. He paused with his foot on the first step, as he had done before, turned to the owner, and said:

"No particular hurry about reaching Corea, is there?"

"Why?" asked Hemster shortly.

"Well, you see, sir, I don't want to run down and sink one of them there little islands in the Archipelago, and have a suit for damages against me; so, unless you're in a hurry I propose to run a couple of hundred miles west, and then north this side of the hundred-and-twenty-fifth meridian."

"Washington or Greenwich?" asked the owner.

"Well, sir," said the captain with a smile, "I'm not particular, so long as there's a clear way ahead of me. I once sailed with a Dutchman who worked on the meridian of Ferro, which is the westernmost point of the Canary Islands. When I am in home waters of course I work by Washington, but the charts I've got for this region is Greenwich, and so I say the hundred-and-twenty-fifth."

"That's all right," replied Hemster seriously. "I thought you were too patriotic a man to use any meridian but our own, and then I thought you were so polite you were using Greenwich out of compliment to Mr. Tremorne here. You pick out the meridian that has the fewest islands along it and fewest big waves, and you'll satisfy me."

The owner said all this quite seriously, and I perceived he had a sense of humour which at first I had not given him credit for.

The captain laughed good-naturedly and disappeared. Mr. Hemster and I finished our dinner together in silence, then went on deck and had coffee and cigars. Although he proffered wine and liqueurs he never drank any spirits himself. I was able to help him out in that direction, as he once drily remarked.

It was one of the most beautiful evenings I had ever witnessed. There was no breeze except the gentle current caused by the motion of the yacht. The sea was like glass, and as night fell the moon rose nearly at the full. Mr. Hemster retired early, as I afterward learned was his custom, but whether to work in his office or to sleep in his bed I never knew. He seemed to have no amusement except the eternal rolling of the unlit cigar in his lips. Although there was a good library on board I never saw him open a book or display the slightest interest in anything pertaining to literature, science, or art. This is a strange world, and in spite of his undoubted wealth I experienced a feeling of pity for him, and I have not the slightest doubt he entertained the same feeling toward me.

I went forward after my employer left me, and asked the captain if outsiders were permitted on the bridge, receiving from him a cordial invitation to ascend. He had a wooden chair up there in which he sat, tilted back against the after rail of the bridge, while his crossed feet were elevated on the forward one, and in this free and easy attitude was running the ship. Of course there was nothing calling for exceeding vigilance, because the great watery plain, bounded by the far-off, indistinct horizon, was absolutely empty, and the yacht jogged along at an easy pace, which, as I have said, gave one the impression that much power was held in reserve. I sat on the forward rail opposite him, and listened to his stories, which were often quaint and always good. He had been a fisherman on the banks of Newfoundland in his early days, and his droll characterization of the men he had met were delicious to listen to. From the very first day I admired the captain, whose name I never learned, and this admiration increased the more I knew of him. I often wonder if he is still following the sea, and indeed I can never imagine him doing anything else. He was able, efficient, and resourceful; as capable a man as it was ever my fortune to meet.

My interest in the captain's stories came to an abrupt conclusion when I saw a lady emerge from the companion-way, look anxiously around for a moment, and then begin a slow promenade up and down the after deck. I bade good-night to the captain, and descended from the bridge. The lady paused as she saw me approach, and I thought for a moment she was about to retreat. But she did not do so. I had determined to speak to Miss Hemster on the first opportunity as if nothing had occurred. Ill-will is bad enough in any case, but nowhere is it more deplorable than on shipboard, because people have no escape from one another there. I was resolved that so far as I was concerned there should not be a continuance of the estrangement, which must affect more or less each one in our company, unless it was the captain, who seemed a true philosopher, taking whatever came with equal nonchalance. As I neared the lady, however, I saw she was not Gertrude Hemster, but Hilda Stretton.

" It is a lovely evening, Miss Stretton," I ventured to say, " and I am glad to see you on deck to enjoy it."

" I came up for a breath of fresh air," she replied simply, with no enthusiasm for the loveliness of the night, which I had just been extolling. I surmised instinctively that she preferred to be alone, and was inwardly aware that the correct thing for me to do was to raise my yachting-cap and pass on, for she had evidently come to a standstill in her promenade, to give me no excuse for joining it. But, whether or not it was the glamour of the moonlight, her face was much more attractive than it had seemed when, for the first time, I had had a glimpse of it, and, be that as it may, I say this in excuse for my persistence. When has a young man ever been driven from his purpose by the unresponsiveness of the lady he is bold enough to address?

" If you do not mind, Miss Stretton, I should be very much gratified if you would allow me to join your evening saunter."

" The deck belongs as much to you as it does to me," was her cold rejoinder, " and I think I should tell you I am but the paid servant of its actual owner."

I laughed, more to chase away her evident embarrassment than because there was anything really to laugh about. I have noticed that a laugh sometimes drives away restraint. It is the most useful of human ejaculations, and often succeeds where words would fail.

"A warning in exchange for your warning!" I exclaimed as cheerfully as I could. "I, too, am a paid servant of the owner of this yacht."

"I did not expect to hear the cousin of Lord Tremorne admit as much," she replied, thawing somewhat.

"Well, you have just heard the cousin of his lordship do so, and I may add on behalf of Lord Tremorne that if he were in my place I know his candour would compel him to say the same thing."

"Englishmen think themselves very honest, do they not?" she commented, somewhat ungraciously, it seemed to me, for after all I was trying to make conversation, always a difficult task when there is veiled opposition.

"Oh, some Englishmen are honest, and some are not, as is the case with other nationalities. I don't suppose a dishonest Englishman would have any delusions about the matter, and perhaps if you pressed him he would admit his delinquency. I hope you are not prejudiced against us as a nation; and, if you are, I sincerely trust you will not allow any impression you may have acquired regarding myself to deepen that prejudice, because I am far from being a representative Englishman."

We were now walking up and down the deck together, but her next remark brought me to an amazed standstill.

"If you possess the candour with which you have just accredited yourself and your people, you would have said that you hoped I was not prejudiced against your nation, but you were certain, if such unfortunately was the case, the charm of your manner and the delight of your conversation would speedily remove it."

"Good gracious, Miss Stretton," I cried, " do you take me for a conceited ass?"

The lady condescended to laugh a little, very low and very sweetly, but it was an undeniable laugh, and so I was grateful for it.

"You mistake me," she said. "I took you for a superior person, that was all, and I think superior persons sometimes make mistakes."

"What mistake have I fallen into, if you will be so good as to tell me?"

"Well, as a beginning, Mr. Tremorne, I think that if I was an English lady you would not venture to accost me as you have done to-night, without a proper introduction."

"I beg your pardon. I considered myself introduced to you by Miss Hemster to-day at luncheon; and if our host had not so regarded it, I imagine he would have remedied the deficiency."

" Mr. Hemster, with a delicacy which I regret to say seems to be unappreciated, knowing me to be a servant in his employ, did not put upon me the embarrassment of an introduction."

"Really, Miss Stretton, I find myself compelled to talk to you rather seriously," said I, with perhaps a regrettable trace of anger in my voice. "You show yourself to be an extremely ignorant young woman."

Again she laughed very quietly.

"Oh!" she cried, with an exultation that had hitherto been absent from her conversation; "the

66

veneer is coming off, and the native Englishman stands revealed in the moonlight."

"You are quite right, the veneer is coming off. And now, if you have the courage of your statements, you will hear the truth about them. On the other hand, if you like to say sharp things and then run away from the consequences, there is the saloon, or there is the other side of the deck. Take your choice."

"I shall borrow a piece of English brag and say I am no coward. Go on."

"Very well. I came down from the bridge after a most friendly and delightful talk with the captain, having no other thought in my mind than to make myself an agreeable comrade to you when I saw you on deck."

"That was a very disingenuous beginning for a truthful lecture, Mr. Tremorne. When you saw me, you thought it was Miss Hemster, and you found out too late that it was I; so you approached me with the most polite and artful covering of your disappointment."

We were walking up and down the deck again, and took one or two turns before I spoke once more.

"Yes, Miss Stretton, you are demoniacally right. I shall amend the beginning of my lecture, then, by alluding to an incident which I did not expect to touch upon. At luncheon Miss Hemster received my greeting with what seemed to me unnecessary insolence. We are to be housed together for some time aboard this yacht; therefore I came down to greet her as if the incident to which I have alluded had not taken place."

67

"How very good of you!" said Miss Stretton sarcastically.

"Madam, I quite agree with you. Now we will turn to some of your own remarks, if you don't mind. In the first place, you said I would not address an English lady to whom I had not been properly introduced. In that statement you were entirely wrong. Five years ago, on an Atlantic liner, I, without having been introduced, asked the Countess of Bayswater to walk the deck with me, and she graciously consented. Some time after that, the deck steward being absent, her Grace the Duchess of Pentonville, without a formal introduction to me, asked me to tuck her up in her steamer chair; then she requested me to sit down beside her, which I did, and we entered into the beginning of a very pleasant acquaintance which lasted during the voyage."

"Dear me!" said Miss Stretton, evidently unimpressed, "how fond you are of citing members of the nobility!"

"Many of them are, or have been, friends of my own; so why should I not cite them? However, my object was entirely different. If I had said that Mrs. Jones or Mrs. Smith were the people in question, you might very well have doubted that they were ladies, and so my illustration would have fallen to the ground. You said English ladies, and I have given you the names of two who are undoubtedly ladies, and undoubtedly English, for neither of them is an American who has married a member of our nobility."

If ever fire flashed from a woman's eyes, it was upon

this occasion. Miss Stretton's face seemed transformed with anger.

"Sir!" she flashed, "that last remark was an insult to my countrywomen, and was intended as such. I bid you good-night, and I ask you never to speak to me again."

"Exactly as I thought," said I; "the moment shells begin to fly, you beat a retreat."

Miss Stretton had taken five indignant steps toward the companion-way when my words brought her to a standstill. After a momentary pause she turned around with a proud motion of her figure which elicited my utmost admiration, walked back to my side, and said very quietly:

"Pardon me; pray proceed."

"I shall not proceed, but shall take the liberty of pausing for a moment to show you the futility of jumping to a conclusion. Now, try to comprehend. You said, *English* ladies. My illustration would have been useless if the Countess and the Duchess had been Americans. Do you comprehend that, or are you too angry?"

I waited for a reply but none came.

"Let me tell you further," I went on, "that I know several American women who possess titles; and if any man in my presence dared to hint that one or other of them was not a lady I should knock him down if I could, and if no one but men were about. So you see I was throwing no disparagement on your countrywomen, but was merely clenching my argument on the lines you yourself had laid down."

"I see; I apologize. Pray go on with the lecture."

"Thank you for the permission, and on your part please forgive any unnecessary vehemence which I have imported into what should be a calm philosophical pronouncement. When you accuse an Englishman of violating some rule of etiquette, he is prone to resent such an imputation, partly because he has an uneasy feeling that it may be true. He himself admits that nearly every other nation excels his in the arts of politeness. It is really not at all to his discredit that he fondly hopes he has qualities of heart and innate courtesy which perhaps may partly make up for his deficiency in outward suavity of manner. Now, madam, etiquette is elastic. It is not an exact science, like mathematics. The rules pertaining to decimal fractions are the same the world over, but the etiquette of the Court differs from the etiquette of the drawing-room, and dry-land etiquette differs from the etiquette on board ship."

"I don't see why it should," interrupted Miss Stretton.

"Then, madam, it shall be my privilege to explain. Imagine us cast on a desert shore. If, for instance, our captain were less worthy than he is, and ran us on the rocks of Quelpaerd Island, which is some distance ahead of us, you would find that all etiquette would disappear."

"Why?"

"Why? Because we should each have to turn around and mutually help the others. Whether I had been introduced to you or not, I should certainly endeavour to provide you with food and shelter; whereas if I contracted one of the island's justly celebrated fevers, your good heart would prompt you to do what you could for my restoration. Now a ship is but a stepping-stone between the mainland of civilization and the desert island of barbarism. This fact, unconsciously or consciously, seems to be recognized, and so the rules of etiquette on board ship relax, and I maintain, with the brutal insistance of my race, that I have not infringed upon them." .

"I think that is a very capital and convincing illustration, Mr. Tremorne," confessed the lady generously.

Now, look you, how vain a creature is man. That remark sent a glow of satisfaction through my being such as I had not experienced since a speech of my youth was applauded by my fellow-students at the Union in Oxford. Nevertheless, I proceeded stubbornly with my lecture, which I had not yet finished.

"Now, madam, I am going to give you the opportunity to charge me with inconsistency. I strenuously object to the application of the term 'servant' as applied to yourself or to me. I am not a servant."

"But, Mr. Tremorne, you admitted it a while ago, and furthermore said that your distinguished cousin would also have confessed as much if in your place."

"I know I said so; but that was before the veneer fell away."

"Then what becomes of the candour of which you boasted? Has it gone with the veneer?"

"They are keeping each other company on the ocean

some miles behind us. I have thrown them overboard."

Miss Stretton laughed with rather more of heartiness than she had yet exhibited.

"Well, I declare," she cried; "this is a transformation scene, all in the moonlight!"

"No, I am not Mr. Hemster's servant. Mr. Hemster desires to use my knowledge of the Eastern languages and my experience in Oriental diplomacy.
For this he has engaged to pay, but I am no more his
servant than Sir Edward Clark is a menial to the client
who pays him for the knowledge he possesses; and,
if you will permit me the English brag, which you
utilized a little while since, I say I am a gentleman and
therefore the equal of Mr. Silas K. Hemster, or any one
else."

"You mean superior, and not equal."

"Madam, with all due respect, I mean nothing of
the sort."

"Nevertheless, that is what is in your mind and in
your manner. By the way, is your lecture completed?"

"Yes, entirely so. It is your innings now. You
have the floor, or the deck rather."

"Then I should like to say that Silas K. Hemster,
as you call him, is one of the truest gentlemen that
ever lived."

"Is n't that his name?"

"You were perfectly accurate in naming him, but
you were certainly supercilious in the tone in which
you named him."

A CHICAGO PRINCESS

"Oh, I say!"

"No, you don't; it is *my* say, if you please."

"Certainly, certainly; but at first you try to make me out a conceited ass, and now you endeavour to show that I am an irredeemable cad. I have the utmost respect for Mr. Hemster."

"Have you? Well, I am very glad to hear it, and I wish to give you a firmer basis for that opinion than you have been able to form from your own observation. Mr. Hemster may not be learned in books, but he is learned in human nature. He is the best of men, kind, considerate, and always just. He was a lifelong friend of my father, now, alas, no more in life. They were schoolboys together. It was inevitable that Mr. Hemster should become very wealthy, and equally inevitable that my father should remain poor. My father was a dreamy scholar, and I think you will admit that he was a gentleman, for he was a clergyman of the Episcopal Church. He was not of the money-making order of men, and, if he had been, his profession would have precluded him from becoming what Mr. Hemster is. Although Mr. Hemster grew very rich, it never in the least interfered with his friendship for my father nor with his generosity to my father's child. If I cared to accept that generosity it would be unstinted. As it is, he pays me much more than I am worth. He is simple and honest, patient and kind. Patient and kind," she repeated, with a little tremor of the voice that for a moment checked her utterance,—"a true gentleman, if ever there was one."

"My dear Miss Stretton," I said, "what you say of

him is greatly to the credit of both yourself and Mr. Hemster; but it distresses me that you should intimate that I have failed to appreciate him. He has picked me up, as I might say, from the gutters of Nagasaki without even a line of recommendation or so much as a note of introduction."

"That is what I said to you; he is a judge of men rather than of literature and the arts; and it is entirely to your credit that he has taken you without credentials. You may be sure, were it otherwise, I should not have spent so much time with you as I have done this evening. But his quick choice should have given you a better insight into his character than that which you possess?"

"There you go again, Miss Stretton. What have I said or done which leads you to suppose I do not regard Mr. Hemster with the utmost respect?"

"It is something exceedingly difficult to define. It cannot be set down as lucidly as your exposition of etiquette. It was your air, rather than your manner at luncheon time. It was a very distant and exalted air, which said as plainly as words that you sat down with a company inferior to yourself."

I could not help laughing aloud; the explanation was absolutely absurd.

"Why, my dear Miss Stretton, if I may call you so, you never even glanced at me during luncheon time; how, then, did you get such extraordinary notions into your head?"

"One did not need to glance at you to learn what I have stated. Now, during our conversation you have

74

been frightened—no, that is not the word—you have been surprised — into a verbal honesty that has been unusual to you. Please make the confession complete, and admit that in your own mind you have not done justice to Mr. Hemster."

" Miss Stretton, the word you have been searching for is 'bluff.' I have been bluffed into confessions, before now, which in my calmer moments I regretted. You see I have been in America myself, and 'bluff' is an exceedingly expressive word. And, madam, permit me to say that in this instance the bluff will not work. You cannot get me to admit that either by look or tone I think anything but what is admirable of Mr. Hemster."

" Oh, dear, oh, dear ! " cried the girl in mock despair. It was really wonderful how unconsciously friendly she had become after our tempestuous discussion. " Oh, dear, oh, dear ! how you are fallen from the state of generous exaltation that distinguished you but a short time ago. Please search the innermost recesses of your mind, and tell me if you do not find there something remotely resembling contempt for a man who accepted you — appalling thought ! — without even a note of introduction."

" Very well, my lady, I shall make the search you· recommend. Now we will walk quietly up and down the deck without a word being said by either of us, and during that time I shall explore those recesses of my mind, which no doubt you regard as veritable ' chambers of horrors.' "

We walked together under the bridge, and then to

the very stern of the ship, coming back to the bridge again. As we turned, the lady by my side broke the contract.

"Oh!" she cried with a little gasp, "there is Miss Hemster!"—and I saw the lady she mentioned emerge from the companion-way to the deck.

"Damnation!" I muttered, under my breath, forgetting for an instant in whose presence I stood, until she turned her face full upon me.

"I—I beg your pardon most sincerely," I stammered.

"And I grant it with equal sincerity," she whispered, with a slight laugh, which struck me as rather remarkable, for she had previously become deeply offended at sayings much milder than my surprised ejaculation.

CHAPTER VII

WE were sailing due west, so that the full moon partly revealed the side face of the figure approaching us, and I venture to assert that the old moon, satellite of lovers, never shone upon anything more graceful than the vision we now beheld. Man as I was, I knew intuitively that she was dressed with a perfection far beyond my powers of description. The partly revealed face wore an expression of childlike simplicity and innocence, with all of a mature woman's exquisite beauty. No frowns now marred that smooth brow; the daintily chiseled lips were animated by a smile of supreme loveliness.

"What a perfectly enchanting night!" she cried, as she came to a standstill before us. "But don't you think it is a trifle chilly?"—and a slight shiver vibrated her frame. "But I suppose you have been energetically walking, and therefore have not noticed the change of temperature. Oh, Hilda, darling, would you mind running down to my room and bringing up that light fleecy wrap, which I can thrown over my shoulders?"

"I will bring it at once," replied Miss Stretton, hastening toward the companion-way. Just as she reached the head of the stair a ripple of tinkling laughter added music to the night.

" Dear me, how stupid I am ! " cried Miss Hemster, " Why, Hilda, I have it here on my arm all the time ! Don't bother, darling ! "

Miss Stretton paused for a moment, then said, " Good-night ! " and disappeared down the stairway.

Man is a stupid animal. I did not know at the moment, nor did I learn until long after,— and even then it was a lady who told me,— that this was a sweet dismissal, as effective as it was unperceived by myself.

Miss Hemster busied herself with the fleecy wrap, whose folds proved so unmanageable that I ventured to offer my aid and finally adjusted the fabric upon her shapely shoulders. We began walking up and down the deck, she regulating her step to mine, and, in the friendly manner of yesterday afternoon, placing her hand within my arm.

However, she did not hop and skip along the deck as she had done on the streets of Nagasaki, although I should have thought the smooth white boards offered an almost irresistible temptation to one who had shown herself to be bubbling over with the joy of youth and life. Notwithstanding the taking of my arm, she held herself with great dignity, her head erect and almost thrown back, so I expected to be treated to a new phase of her most interesting character. I was finding it somewhat bewildering, and hardly knew how to begin the conversation ; but whether it was the springing step, or the smoothness of the deck, or both combined, it struck me all at once that she must be a superb dancer, and I was about to make inquiry as to this when she withdrew her hand rather quickly after we had taken two or three turns up and down the deck in silence, and said:

"You are not taking advantage of the opportunity I have been kind enough to present to you."

"What opportunity?" I asked in amazement.

"The opportunity to apologize to me."

"To apologize?" cried I, still more at a loss to understand her meaning. "Pray, for what should I apologize?"

She said with great decision and some impatience:

"How terribly dense you Englishmen are!"

"Yes, I admit it. We are celebrated as a nation for obtuseness. But won't you take pity on this particular Englishman, and enlighten him regarding his offence. What should I apologize for?"

"Why, you told my father you were not a friend of the Mikado!"

"Certainly I told him so. I am not a friend of the Mikado; therefore why should I claim to be?"

"Oh!" she cried, with a fine gesture of disdain, "you are trying to do the George Washington act!"

"The George Washington act!" I repeated.

"Certainly. Of course you don't see that. He could not tell a lie, you know."

"Ah, I understand you. No, I am doing the Mark Twain act. I can tell a lie, but I won't."

"Not even for me?" she asked, looking up at me with that winning smile of hers.

"Ah, when you put it that way I fear I shall be unable to emulate the truthfulness of either George **or** Mark."

" Now that is n't so bad," she said, taking my arm again, which gave me the hope that I had been at least partially restored to favour.

" You certainly intimated to me yesterday that you were a friend of the Mikado."

" Then I am to blame; for with equal certainty I had no right to do so."

" You said you had seen him several times and had spoken with him."

" Yes, but that does not constitute a claim upon His Majesty's consideration."

" Why, you have only seen me two or three times, and I am sure you know I 'm a friend of yours."

" Madam, I am delighted to hear you say so. If the Mikado had made a similar statement, I should claim him as a friend before all the world."

" Then there was another thing you said, and I suppose you 'll go back on that, too. You said you were a partisan of mine, or, since you are such a stickler for accuracy, an adherent—I think that was the word— yes, you were my adherent, or retainer, or something of the sort, such as we read of in old-fashioned novels, and when you said so, poor little trustful girl that I am, I believed you."

" Indeed, Miss Hemster, you had every right to do so. Should occasion arise, you will find me your staunch defender."

" Oh, that 's all very pretty; but when it comes to the test, then you fail. You heard what my father said.

You must have known I meant you to claim friendship with the Mikado. Poor father's as transparent as glass, and he surely made it as plain as this funnel that I wished you to claim friendship with the head of the Japanese nation. So, after all your beautiful promises, the moment you get a chance to back me up, you do so by going back on me."

"My dear Miss Hemster, why did you not give me a hint of your wishes? If, when we were in Nagasaki, you had but said that you wished me to proclaim myself the Emperor's brother, I should have perjured myself on your behalf like a gentleman."

"It happened that I was not on deck when you came aboard, and so did not see you. But I do think, if you had n't forgotten me entirely, you would have learned at once from my father's talk what I wished you to say."

"Yes, I see it all now, when it is too late; but as you have remarked, and as I have admitted, I am extremely dense, and unless a thing is as plain as the funnel—to use your own simile—I am very apt to overlook it. Sometimes I don't see it even then. For instance, when you are walking by my side, I am just as likely to run into the funnel as to walk past it."

She laughed most good naturedly at this observation, and replied:

"Oh, you do say things very charmingly, and I will forgive you, even if you refuse to apologize."

"But I don't refuse to apologize. I *do* apologize—most abjectly—for my stupidity."

"Oh, well, that's all right. Perhaps, when every-

thing 's said and done, it was my own fault in not giving you warning. Next time I want you to stand by
me, I 'll have it all typewritten nice and plain, and will
hand the paper to you twenty-four hours ahead."

"That would be very kind of you, Miss Hemster;
and, besides, you would then possess documentary evidence of the stupidity of an Englishman."

"Oh, we don't need to have documentary evidence
for that," she replied brightly; "but I tell you I was
mad clear through when I knew what you had said to
my father. I raised storm enough to sink the yacht."

"Did you?"

"Did n't I? Why, you *knew* I did."

"I had n't the slightest suspicion of it."

"Oh, well, you are denser than I thought. And I
have been worrying myself all the afternoon for fear
you were offended by the way I told you to take your
seat at the table."

"Offended? I should n't have had the presumption
to think of such a thing. Indeed, it was very kind of
you to indicate my place. Such instructions are usually given by the steward."

She bestowed a sly, sidelong glance upon me, and
there was a somewhat uncertain smile at the corners of
her pretty lips.

"Is that a little dig at me?" she asked.

"Nothing of the sort. It was a mere statement of
fact."

"Sometimes I think," she said meditatively, more to
herself than to me, "that you are not such a fool as
you look."

I was compelled to laugh at this, and replied with as much urbanity as I could call to my command:

"I am overjoyed to hear that statement. It seems to prove that I am making progress. Such evidence always encourages a man."

"Oh, well," she said, with a shrug of impatience, "don't let's talk any more about it. I didn't want to go to Corea, and I *did* want to return to Yokohama; so here we are going to Corea. Don't you think I am a very good-natured girl to let bygones be bygones so easily?"

"You certainly are."

"Then that's settled. Tell me what Miss Stretton was talking to you about."

I was somewhat taken aback by this extraordinary request, but replied easily:

"Oh, we had not been walking the deck very long, and we discussed nothing of extreme importance so far as I can remember."

"What did she say about me?"

"I assure you, Miss Hemster, your name was not mentioned between us."

"Really? Then what on earth *did* you talk about?"

"When I have the good fortune to be in your presence, Miss Hemster, I confess it seems impossible that I should talk about anyone else than yourself, nevertheless I should not presume to discuss one lady with another."

The girl jerked away her arm again, and turned to me with a flash in her eyes that was somewhat disconcerting.

"Look here, Mr. Tremorne," she cried, "if you've got anything to say against me, I want you to say it right out like a man, and not to hint at it like a spiteful woman."

"What have I said now?" I inquired very humbly.

"You know quite well what you have said. But if you imagine I am as stupid as you admit yourself to be, you'll get left!"

"My dear madam," I ventured; "one of the advantages of having a thick skin is that a person does not take offence where no offence is meant."

"There you go again! You know very well that you were driving at me when you said that you refused to discuss one lady with another; because, if you meant anything at all, you meant that I was trying to do what you couldn't bring yourself to do; and when you talk of 'lady' and 'lady' you are in effect putting Miss Stretton on an equality with me."

"I should never think of doing so," I replied, with a bow to the angry person beside me.

"Is that another?" she demanded. "Oh, you know very well what I mean. Do you consider Miss Stretton a lady?"

"My acquaintance with her is of the shortest, yet I should certainly call her a lady."

, , "Then what do you call me?"

"A lady also."

"Well, if that isn't putting us on an equality, what is?"

"I said, madam, that I did not put you on an equality. That was done by a celebrated document which you often fling in our faces. I refer to the Declaration of Independence, which, if I remember rightly, begins—'All men are created equal,' and I suppose, as the humourist puts it, that the men embrace the women."

"Miss Stretton is my paid servant," insisted Miss Hemster, evading the point; "and, as was said in the opera of 'Pinafore,' when one person has to obey the orders of another, equality is out of the question."

"I did n't think that made any difference in the United States."

"But this is n't the United States."

"I beg your pardon, but this is the United States. We are on the high seas, aboard a steamer that is registered in New York, and so this deck is just as much a part of your country as is New York itself, and the laws of the United States would justify the captain in putting me in irons if he thought my conduct deserved such treatment."

"Then you refuse to tell me what you and Miss Stretton were discussing!"

"My dear madam, if Miss Stretton asked me what you and I were discussing, I should certainly refuse to inform her. Should I not be justified in doing so? I leave it to yourself. Would you be pleased if I repeated our conversation to Miss Stretton?"

"Oh, I don't know that I should mind," replied Miss Hemster mildly, the storm subsiding as quickly as it had risen; "I have no doubt she told you that her father was a clergyman, and that my father had borrowed five hundred dollars from her father to get his start in life. And she doubtless hinted that her father was the founder of our fortune."

"I assure you, Miss Hemster, that she said nothing at all about five hundred dollars or any other sum. She spoke mostly of your father, and she spoke very highly of him."

"She certainly had every right to do so. My father gave her what education she has and supported her ever since."

I made no comment upon this statement, and my companion veered round a bit and said brightly:

"Oh, I see you don't like me to talk like that, and perhaps I should n't, but Hilda Stretton is as sly as they make them, and I 've no doubt she came on deck just to size you up, while you would never suspect it."

"I venture to think you do the young lady an injustice, Miss Hemster. I am sure she would have preferred to walk the deck alone, although she was too polite to say so. I rather fear I forced my company upon her."

"Oh, yes, oh, yes; I understand all about that. Such is just the impression Hilda Stretton would like to make upon a man. Now I am honest. I came on deck purposely to have a talk with you."

"Then I am very much flattered."

"Well, you ought to be, and I may say this for you, that you don't talk to me in the least as other men do. Nobody has ever dared to contradict me."

"Have I done so? You shock me, for I certainly did not intend to contradict you."

"Why, you have done nothing else, and I don't

think it's gentlemanly at all. But we'll let that go. Now I wish to talk about yourself."

" Well, I think we might choose a more entertaining topic."

" We'll talk about Lord Tremorne then."

" Hang Lord Tremorne! "

" Ah, Miss Stretton and you were discussing him then? "

" Indeed we were not, but I am rather tired of the gentleman. Yet he is a very good fellow, and I ought not to say ' Hang him! ' even if I am on the high seas. I am sure I wish him nothing but good."

" If he were to die, would you become Lord Tremorne? "

" Bless me, no! "

" Who stands between you? "

" His three sons, who are very healthy specimens of humanity, I am glad to say."

" Isn't there ever any possibility of your becoming Lord Tremorne, then? "

" Oh, there's a possibility of anything, but no probability. I may say quite truthfully that no one would be so sorry as I if the probability occurred."

" Don't you want to have a title? "

" I wouldn't give twopence for it."

" Really? I thought every one in England wanted a title? "

" Dear me, no! There are men in England, plain Mr. This or That, who wouldn't change their appellation for the highest title that could be offered them."

" Why? "

"Oh, they belong to fine old families and look upon the newer aristocracy as upstarts."

"It seems funny to talk of old families, for all families are the same age. We all spring from Adam, I suppose."

"Doubtless, but I believe the College of Arms does not admit such a contention."

"Don't you think family pride a very idiotic thing?"

"Oh, I don't know. To tell you the truth, I have n't thought very much about it, though I don't see why we should parade the pedigree of a horse and be ashamed of the pedigree of a man."

"It is n't the same thing. A horse may have notable ancestors, whereas I am told that most of your aristocracy sprang from thieves and outlaws."

"As far as that goes, some of them are still in the pirate profession, those who belong to the public companies, for example,— bogus companies, I mean. I suppose, after all said and done, that the pedigree of even the oldest family in Europe is as nothing to that of the Eastern Kings, for this King of Corea that we are going to see traces his ancestry about as far back as did Pooh-Bah."

"Do you think there will be any trouble in getting to see his Corean Majesty?" Miss Hemster asked with a shade of anxiety in her tone.

"I am not at all sure, for the etiquette of the Corean Court is very rigid. A horseman must dismount when he is passing the Palace, although it is but a ramshackle conglomeration of shabbiness. Every one ad-

88

mitted to the Presence must prostrate himself before the King."

" Well, I shan't do it," said the girl confidently.

" I hope to obtain a relaxation of the rule in the case of a Princess like yourself, Miss Hemster. If his Majesty should graciously touch your hand, the law of Corea demands that ever afterward you must wear a badge as token of the distinction conferred upon you."

" Oh, I shall just wear another ring with the arms of Corea on it,—that is, if Corea has arms,"—said Miss Hemster with vivacity. " I am sure it is very good of you to take all this trouble for us. And now I must bid you good-night and thank you for the very pleasant walk we have had together."

With that my lady withdrew her bright presence and disappeared down the companion-way.

CHAPTER VIII

I AWOKE next morning after a sweet and dreamless sleep that was almost inspiring. Months and months had passed since I slept in a European bed, and, although necessity had accustomed me to the habit of a Japanese mat upon the floor and a block of wood for a pillow, I must confess that the bed of the West still seemed to me a very paradise of luxury. There were more patent contrivances about that yacht than I have ever seen in such small compass before. Of course it had electric lights everywhere. There was a water-condensing machine, an ice-making machine, and all the usual fittings that now go to the construction of a luxurious steamer for sailing in warm latitudes. There was a bathroom which was Oriental in its splendour and Occidental in its patent fittings. One could have any sort of bath that one desired. By simply turning a handle on a dial the great marble basin became filled with water at any temperature indicated by the figures at which you set the pointer, from boiling-hot to ice-cold. This was indeed a delight, and when I came to it from my room in dressing-gown and slippers I found the Japanese boy there with a cup of delicious tea such as can be had only in the immediate vicinity of China. On a dainty plate whose figure work was only partially obscured by a filmy lace napkin were some finger-lengths and finger-widths of buttered toast. "Rupert, my boy," I said to myself, "you have indeed fallen upon your feet!"

I now knew that I was going to have the pleasantest voyage of my life   The clouds which yesterday threatened to obscure my acquaintance with Miss Hemster had cleared away, and although I had surmised that the young woman was somewhat quick to take offence when one approached the confines of either ridicule or criticism, yet I was well aware that no man has a right to inflict conversation that is distasteful upon any woman, and I thought I had sufficient power over my speech to prevent further errors in that direction.   A most unaccustomed sense of elation filled me, and, as I tossed about my wardrobe, I came across a pair of Oxford bags that I had not worn for years. As they were still spotlessly white, I put them on, with a blazer which gave to the world the somewhat glaring colors of my college, and, thus gloriously arrayed with cap on head, I almost imagined myself about to stroll along the High, once more an extremely young man.

My costume made quite a sensation at the breakfast-table, and caused great laughter on the part of our worthy captain, who said the only thing it reminded him of was a clown in Barnum's circus. Miss Hemster was good enough to compliment the outfit, and, after the meal was over, did me the honour of strolling up and down the deck for nearly an hour, after which she disappeared below. Silas K. Hemster occupied his customary place on deck in the wicker armchair, and

after his daughter had deserted me I stood beside him
for a few moments, endeavouring to engage him in
conversation, but soon saw that he preferred his own
thoughts, for which preference, to be sure, I could find
no fault with him, for anything I had to say was
neither novel nor entertaining. I was about to go
below and select a book from the rather extensive
library when there met me at the head of the companion-way the notes of the very subdued playing of one of
Chopin's most charming nocturnes. I paused for a
moment at the head of the stair, then descended softly,
saying to myself that Miss Hemster was a most accomplished musician.

Perhaps I have not stated that at the farther end of
the saloon from the foot of the stairs stood an excellent
piano, and at the stairway end an equally fine American organ. As I descended I soon saw that the musician was Miss Stretton, who sat with her back
toward me, playing with a touch I have seldom heard
equalled even by professionals. I am very fond of
music, so I slipped quietly into a chair and listened to
those divine harmonies divinely played. Miss Stretton
went on from nocturne to nocturne, and I felt somewhat guilty at thus surreptitiously listening, but resolved that the moment she gave a sign of ceasing I
would steal quietly up the stair again without revealing
my presence.

Down the passage facing me, that formed a high-
way from the saloon to the suites occupied by the ladies, I saw Miss Hemster come out of her room, and,
by the same token, she must have seen me. She ad-

vanced a few steps, then stood still, apparently listening to the music, finally turned, and re-entered her apartment with a distinct, emphatic slam of the door. I paid no attention to this, but then was the time for me to steal on deck again if I had had any wisdom in my head, which I so frequently must admit I have not. Miss Stretton, absorbed in the music, presumably had not heard the slam of the door, but a little later Miss Hemster emerged again, and this time came straight down the passage and through the saloon, with a swish, swish of silken skirts that sounded eloquent in anger. I have never heard silk skirts rustle since then without remembering the occasion I am endeavouring to describe; yet never before or since have I heard the hiss of silk that actually swore, if I may be permitted the use of such an expression.

The young woman marched past me with head erect, and a gleam in her eyes such as I had seen on one occasion before, but this time fixed and anything but transient, as the other flash had been. I rose respectfully to my feet as she passed, but she cast not even a glance at me, merely pausing for a second at the foot of the stairs to catch up the train of her magnificent gown, then up the steps she went at a run. Now I had consciously given the girl no cause of annoyance, but, the music having ceased suddenly, I turned around and saw Miss Stretton regarding me with something like dismay in her eyes.

" How long have you been here? " she asked.

" Oh, only for a few minutes," I replied. " Pray go on, Miss Stretton. I am very fond of music, and not for years have I been privileged to hear it so well played."

"It is very kind of you to say that," murmured Hilda Stretton, "but I think I have played enough for one morning."

"At least finish the selection you were just now engaged upon," I begged.

"Some other time, please," she said in a low voice; and I did not urge her further, for I saw she was frightened.

"Very well," I replied, "I shall take that as a promise."

She inclined her head as she came down the room, and went up the stairs, disappearing also on deck, leaving me wondering what all this disquietude was about. I thought of going on deck myself, but, feeling slightly resentful at the treatment accorded me by Miss Hemster, I walked forward, sat down on the piano-stool, and began to drum a few of the catchy London tunes that ran through my head. I was playing "Knocked 'em in the Old Kent Road" with little idea of how excellent an overture it would prove for the act about to be commenced, and was thinking of the Strand, and the Tivoli, and Chevalier, and Piccadilly Circus, and the Empire, and Leicester Square, and the Alhambra, when I was startled by a woman's appealing voice crying just above a whisper:

"Oh, don't, Gertie; please don't!"

I turned my head and saw, coming down the stairway, Gertrude Hemster followed by Hilda Stretton. The latter was evidently almost on the verge of tears,

" Will you stop your foolish pounding on *my* piano ?"

Page 95

but the face of the former was shocking to behold. I could not have believed that a countenance so beautiful was capable of being transformed into a visage that might have stood model for a picture of murderous wrath.

"Will you stop your foolish pounding on *my* piano?" she cried, with a tremendous emphasis on the first personal pronoun.

"Madam, I have stopped," I replied, giving a soft answer that failed to have the supposed effect.

"I guess you think you own the yacht and all it contains, don't you? Now, I beg to inform you that we don't allow employees to conduct themselves as if they were in a bar-room or a drinking-saloon."

As she said this, she strode once up and down the length of the room.

"Madam," said I, "I beg your pardon, and shall never touch your piano again. My only excuse is that I have been so accustomed to public liners, where the piano is free to all, that for the moment I forgot myself."

At this juncture Miss Stretton was so injudicious as to touch the other on the elbow, apparently trying to guide her into the passage that led to her room, but Miss Hemster whirled around like an enraged tigress, and struck her companion a blow that would have landed on her cheek had not the victim suddenly and instinctively raised an arm to protect her face. Then with the viciousness of a harridan of Drury Lane Miss Hemster grasped the shrinking girl by the shoulders, and shook her as a terrier does a rat, finally forcing her down into a seat by the side of the table. One girl's face was as white as paper, and the other's nearly purple with rage. I had intended to go up on deck, but paused for two reasons. First I was afraid of injury to Miss Stretton, and secondly the struggle took place, if struggle it could be called when one was entirely passive, in the midst of the only route open to me.

"You dare to interfere, you little fool," shrieked Miss Hemster. "You that are the cause of all the trouble, with your silly little ditties—tinkle-tinkle-tinkle-tinkle — and I'll box your ears for you if you dare stir!"

"Madam," said I, "you are possibly so ignorant as not to know that you were listening to Chopin's most subtle harmonies."

This had exactly the effect I desired, which was to turn her away from the trembling girl whom she had so harshly misused.

"Ignorant, you puppy! Have you the gall to apply such language to me, looking, as you do, like a monkey on a stick; like a doll that one can buy at the bargain counter."

This graphic description of my Oxford blazer was so striking that in spite of the seriousness of the case I did the one thing I should not have done,—I laughed. The laugh was like a spark to a powder-mine, and what made the crisis worse was that the old gentleman in his armchair on deck, hearing the shrieking voice, came down, his face haggard with anxiety.

"Gertie, Gertie!" he cried. I would not like to

say the young lady swore, but she came so near it that there was but tissue paper between the expression she used and that which an angry fish-wife would have employed. With the quickness of light she sprang at a large Japanese vase which temporarily decorated the center of the table. This she heaved up, and with the skill of a football player flung it squarely at me. Now, I have had some experience on the football field myself, and I caught that vase with a dexterity which would have evoked applause had any enthusiast of the game happened to be present. I suppose my placing of this huge vase on the top of the piano was the last straw, or perhaps it was her father coming forward, crying in a grief-shaken voice, " Oh, Gertie, Gertie, my child, my child ! "

I was so sorry for him that I passed him and would have gone on deck out of the way, but my purpose was checked by a startling incident. The young woman had whisked open a drawer. I heard it come clattering to the floor, for she had jerked it clear from its place ; then there was a scream. Turning quickly around I met the blinding flash of a pistol, and heard behind me the crash of a splintering mirror. The sound of the revolver in that contracted space was deafening, and even through the smoke I saw that my young friend was about to fire again. I maintain it was not fear for my own life that caused instant action on my part, but this infuriated creature, who seemed to have become insane in her anger, faced three helpless, unarmed people, and whatever was to be done had to be done quickly. I leaped through the air, and grasped her two wrists with an energetic clutch I daresay she had never encountered before.

" Drop that revolver ! " I cried.

" Let go my wrists, you beast," she hissed in my face. For answer I raised her arms and brought them down with a force that would have broken her fingers with the weight of the revolver if she had not let it go clattering to the floor.

" You beast, you beast, you beast ! " she shrieked at me, as well as her choking throat would allow utterance. I swung her around a quarter-circle, then pushed her back, somewhat rudely I fear, until she sank down into a chair.

" Now, sit there and cool," I cried, giving her a hearty shake, so that she should know how it felt herself. " If you don't keep quiet I 'll box your ears."

I don't defend my action at all; I merely state that I was just as angry as she was, and perhaps a little more so.

" You brute, let go of my wrists ! I 'll kill you for this ! Hilda, call the captain and have this man put in irons. Father, how can you stand there like a coward and see a beastly ruffian use me in this way ? "

" Oh, Gertie, Gertie ! " repeated the father without moving.

She now burst into a passionate flood of tears, and I released her wrists, ready, however, to catch them again if she made any motion to reach the revolver.

During this fierce if brief contest,—it took less time in happening than it requires in telling,—Miss Stretton had been seated in the chair upon which the angry woman had thrust her, and she gazed at us in open-eyed terror. The old man stood half leaning against the table, steadying himself with his hands. Miss Hemster's fit of weeping was as dramatic as everything else she did. It began with a burst of very angry and genuine tears, and this storm passed through a gamut of more or less varying emotions until it subsided into a hysterical half-sobbing, half-gasping wail which resembled the cry of the helpless child who had been tyrannized over. It was bogusly pathetic, but I saw it went straight to the old man's heart and wrung it with very real agony, and this mean advantage which I knew she was taking of the father's deep love for her increased my scornful contempt for the creature. His grief was actual enough, and she was quite consciously playing upon it, although,—wonderful actress that she was,—she pretended an utter abandon of heart-breaking sorrow.

As for me, I undoubtedly felt myself the brute she had named me, and even at that moment,—much more so later,—was shocked to find in my own nature depths of primeval savagery which had hitherto been unsuspected. Seeing, however, that the worst of the storm was over, and that the young woman would make no more attempts at gun-firing, I replaced the drawer in position and threw into it its scattered former contents. Then I picked up the revolver, saying:

" I will keep this, for there is nothing more dangerous than such an instrument in the hands of a woman who can't shoot "

The effect of this remark on the drooping figure

was instantaneous. She abruptly raised her tear-sodden face, which now became crimson with a new wave of anger.

"You gaping baboon," she cried, "I can shoot a great deal better than you can!"

I paid no heed to her, but, advising Mr. Hemster to lock up any other firearms he might have on board, abruptly left the saloon.

CHAPTER IX

I WALKED the deck alone, the revolver stuck between my hip and my gaudy sash, as if I were a veritable pirate, and doubtless my appearance was not dissimilar to some of those nautical heroes who have been terrors of the sea. A pirate more dissatisfied with himself never trod a quarter-deck. If there had been a plank at hand I would willingly have walked it. It was no comfort that I despised the girl, for I despised myself a thousand times more. What right had I to interfere? Why had I not bowed to her when she ordered me away from the piano, and come at once on deck, without proffering any of my foolish explanations? The whole disgraceful row had arisen through my contemptible efforts to justify a situation which allowed of no justification. The piano was hers, as she truly said, and I had no more right to touch it than I had to wear her jewellery. My sole desire at first was to get ashore as soon as anchor was dropped, and never again see either father or daughter. But a few moments' reflection showed me the quandary into which I had brought myself. I was already indebted to the old gentleman, not only for the money he had advanced to me, but for his kindness from the very first, which I had repaid by an interference in his family affairs that made me loathe myself. Never before had I felt so acutely the sting of poverty. Not even in my starvation days at Nagasaki had my lack of means borne so heavily upon me. It was utterly impossible for me to refund a penny of the pounds he had so generously bestowed upon me. The only requital in my power was that of honest service to him, and now I had made my stay on the yacht impossible, when, had I retained a modicum of sanity at the proper moment, I might have withdrawn with no loss of dignity. Now my own self-respect was gone, and I had more than justified every bitter taunt she flung at me.

So, in a very hopeless state of misery and dejection, I walked up and down the deck until Mr. Hemster himself came quietly up the companion-way and took his usual place in his wicker chair, setting his heels upon the rail in front of him, and biting off the end of a cigar. He gave me no greeting, but this also was usual with him, and so it meant nothing one way or another. However, I had at last made up my mind on a course of action, so I strode over to where he sat, and he looked up at me with what I took to be more of apprehension than censure in his gaze. It was no matter of wonder to me that he must be seriously doubting his wisdom in taking on board without recommendation a stranger who had just proved himself such a brawler.

"Mr. Hemster," said I, "an apology is a cheap method of trying to make amends for what is inexcusable; but I should like to tell you, and I should like you to believe, how sorry I am for my conduct of a short time since. I regret to say it is impossible for me to return the money you have advanced. When I first had the pleasure of meeting you, I stated to you quite truthfully that I was at the end of my resources, and of course my prospects have not improved in the mean time, except in so far as your own favour is concerned, and that, I quite realize, I have forfeited. From this time until we sight land, I shall live forward with the crew in the forecastle, and shall not again come aft except in obedience to your orders. When we reach Corea I am entirely at your disposal. If you wish me to carry out the project you have in hand, I shall do so to the best of my ability; if not, I give you my word I will refund to you the money as soon as I can earn it."

"Sit down," he said very quietly, and when I had done so he remained silent, gazing over the rail at the distant horizon for what seemed to me a very long time. Then he spoke, never raising his voice above the level at which he always kept it.

"You are a little excited just now," he said, "and take an exaggerated view of the matter. Do you think any one on deck heard that pistol-shot?"

"I don't know; I rather imagine not. No one seemed at all on the alert when I came up."

"Well, it sounded as if it would raise all creation down below, but perhaps it did n't make such a racket up here. Now, if you went forward and lived with the crew, what would be the effect? They would merely say we made it impossible for you to live aft. I suppose by rights I should n't mind what my crew thinks or says; but I do mind it. We are in a way a small democracy afloat, one man as good as another. If the firing were heard on deck, then the captain will be joking about it at luncheon time, and we 'll know. If it was n't, the least said about it the better. If you don't like to come to meals, I have n't a word to say; you can have them served in your own room. As for the money I advanced, that does n't amount to anything. I am sure you are just the man I want for what there is to do, and when that 's done it will be me that 's owing you money. I 'm a good deal older than you, and I have found that in business a man must keep his temper, or he 's going to give all his adversaries a great advantage over him, and things are cut so close nowadays that no one can afford to give points to his rival. I 've had to control my temper or be a failure, so I controlled it. My daughter has n't had to do that. Instead of blaming her, you should blame me. It 's my temper she 's got."

" My dear Mr. Hemster, I assure you I am blaming neither of you; I am blaming myself."

" Well, that 's all right. It 's a good state of Christian feeling and won't do you any harm. Now you said that when we land you are willing to do anything I ask. Are you willing to do that before we go ashore?"

" Yes, Mr. Hemster, any command you may lay upon me I shall execute without question."

" Oh, I won't lay a command on you at all; but I ask as a favour that you go below, knock at my daughter's door, and tell her you are sorry for what has happened. Put it any way you like, or don't do it at all if you don't want to. After all, she is a woman, you know. You and I are men, and should stand the brunt, even if we are not entitled to it, and it may make things go a little smoother, perhaps."

We are supposed to be an unemotional race, but I confess that the old man's mild words touched me deeply, and made it next to impossible for me to reply to him. But, even so, my own judgment told me that a life of this desire to make things go smoothly had resulted in building up a character in his daughter which took an obstreperous advantage of the kindly old gentleman's strong affection for her. I arose without a word, thrust forward my hand to him, which he shook somewhat shamefacedly, glancing nervously around, fearing there might be onlookers. I entirely appreciated his reserve, and wished for a moment that I had not acted upon my impulse, to his visible embarrassment. I went instantly to the saloon, along the passage, and knocked at the door of Miss Hemster's apartment. She herself opened the door, with what seemed to me to be her usual briskness; but when I looked at her, I saw her drooping like a stricken flower, head bent, and eyes on the floor. Scarcely above a whisper, she asked with tremor-shaken voice:

" Did you wish to see me? "

" Yes, Miss Hemster," I replied, nerving myself to the point. " I wish, since you are good enough to receive me, to apologize most abjectly for my rudeness to you this morning."

She replied in a sad little voice, without looking up:

" I do not really mind in the least how much you play the piano, Mr. Tremorne."

This was so unexpected a remark, so ludicrously aside from the real point at issue between us, so far from touching the hideousness of my culpability, that I looked at the girl, wondering whether or not she was in earnest. I had not come to get permission to play the piano. Her attitude, to which no other word than "wilted" so appropriately applied, continued to be one of mute supplication or dependence. Yet in the semi-darkness I fancied I caught one brief glance at my face. Then she leaned her fair head against the jam of the door and began to cry very softly and very hopelessly.

I stood there like the awkward fool I was, not knowing what to say; and finally she completed my desolation by slowly raising her two arms up toward my face. Since our contest she had removed the striking costume she then wore, and had put on a white lace fleecy garment that was partly dressing-gown, partly tea-gown, decorated with fluttering blue ribbon. This had very wide sleeves which fell away from her arms, leaving them bare and rounded, pure and white. Her two slender, shapely hands hung in helpless fashion from the wrists like lilies on a broken stem. The slow upraising of them seemed to me strange and meaningless, until the light from the inner room fell upon her wrists, and then the purport of her action became stunningly clear to me. Around that dainty forearm, delicately fashioned for the tenderest usage, showed red and angry the marks of my brutal fingers, silent accusers held up before my very eyes. Distraught as I was with self-accusation, I could not help admiring the dramatic effectiveness of the slow motion and resulting attitude. The drooping girl, with her soft, clinging draperies, her sad face so beautiful, her contour so perfect, and those soft appealing hands upraised,— hands that I could not forget had been placed with impulsive friendliness in mine on the streets of Nagasaki,— and all this accompanied by the almost silent symphony of quivering sobs that were little louder than sighs tremulously indrawn, formed a picture that has never been effaced from my memory. I had rather a man's clenched fist had struck me to the ground than that a woman's open palm should be so held in evidence against me. I regard that moment as the most unbearable of my life, and with a cry almost of despair I turned and fled. For once language had become impossible and utterly inadequate.

As I beat this precipitate retreat, was it my overwrought imagination, or was it actual, that I heard an indignant word of expostulation, followed by a low sweet ripple of laughter. Had there been some one else in the room during this painful interview? I staggered like a drunken man up to the deck, and then endeavoured to walk it off and cease thinking.

Mr. Hemster said nothing to me that day, nor I to him, after I came on deck again. For an hour I strode the deck with an energy which, if applied in the right direction, would have driven the yacht faster than she was going. When the gong sounded for luncheon I went down to my own room and was served there. After the meal I did not go up on deck again, but sat on the sofa gloomily smoking. Later I got a novel from the library, and tried to interest myself in it, but failed. I felt physically tired, as if I had done a hard day's work, and, unsentimental as it is to confess it, I fell asleep on the sofa, and slept until the gong for dinner aroused me.

Dinner I also enjoyed in solitary state in my own apartment, then, under the brilliant cluster of electric lights, tried the novel again, but again without success. The nap in the afternoon made sleep improbable if I turned in, so I scarcely knew what to do with myself. I rather envied Silas K. Hemster's reticence, and his seeming dislike for intercourse with his fellows. He was the most self-contained man I had ever met, preferring the communion of his own thoughts to conversation with any one. At this crisis of indecision the way was made plain for me by the youth from Japan. There came a gentle tap at my door, and on opening it the Japanese boy said respectfully:

"Sir, Miss Stretton would like to speak with you on deck."

CHAPTER X

I HAD flung my much-maligned blazer into a corner, and now I slipped on an ordinary tweed coat. I found the deck empty with the exception of Miss Stretton, who was walking up and down in the moonlight, as she had done the night before, but this time she came forward with a sweet smile on her lips, extending her hand to me as if we had been old friends long parted. There was something very grateful to me in this welcome, as I was beginning to look upon myself as a pariah unfit for human companionship. Indeed, I had been bitterly meditating on striking into the Corean wilderness and living hereafter as one of the natives, about the lowest ambition that ever actuated the mind of man.

"Have you sentenced yourself to solitary imprisonment, Mr. Tremorne?"

"Yes. Don't you think I deserve it?"

"Frankly, I don't; but as you did not appear at either luncheon or dinner, and as the Japanese boy who brought my coffee up here told me you were keeping to your room, I thought it as well to send for you, and I hope you are not offended at having your meditation broken in upon. Prisoners, you know, are allowed to walk for a certain time each day in the courtyard.

I do wish I had a ball and chain for your ankles, but we are on board ship, and cannot expect all the luxuries of civilization."

Her raillery cheered me more than I can say.

" Miss Stretton, it is more than good of you to receive an outcast in this generous manner."

" An outcast? Please don't talk rubbish, Mr. Tremorne! Somehow I had taken you for a sensible person, and now all my ideas about you are shattered."

" I don't wonder at it," I said despondently.

" Yes, I know you are in the Slough of Despond, and I am trying to pull you out of it. When I remember that men have ruled great empires, carried on important wars, subdued the wilderness, conquered the ocean, girdled the earth with iron, I declare I wonder where their brains depart to when they are confronted with silly, whimpering, designing women."

" But still, Miss Stretton, to come from the general to the particular, a man has no right to ill-treat a woman."

" I quite agree with you; but, as you say, to come to this particular incident which is in both our minds, do you actually believe that there was ill-treatment? Don't you know in your own soul that if the girl had received treatment like that long ago she would not now be a curse to herself and to all who are condemned to live within her radius?"

" Yet I cannot conceal from myself that it was none of my business. Her father was present, and her correction was his affair."

" Her correction was any one's affair that had the

courage to undertake it. What had you seen? You had seen her strike me, and thrust me from her as if I were a leper. Then you saw this girl with the temper of the—the temper of the—oh, help me——

"Temper of the devil," I responded promptly.

"Thank you! You saw her take up a deadly weapon, and if she has not murdered one of the three of us, we have to thank, not her, but the mercy of God. You did exactly the right thing, and the only thing, and actually she would have admired you for it had it not been that you came down to her door and prostrated yourself for her to trample over you."

"Good heavens, Miss Stretton! were you inside that room?"

"It does n't matter whether I was or not. I know that she twisted you around her little finger, and took her revenge in the only way that was possible for her."

"Ah, but you don't know the depth of my degradation. She showed me her wrists, marked by the fingers of a savage, and that savage was myself."

"Pooh! pooh pooh!" cried Miss Stretton, laughing. "Do you think those marks indicate pain? Not a bit of it. Your grasp of her wrists did not injure her in the least, and, short of putting handcuffs on them, was the only method at your disposal to prevent her perhaps killing her father, a man worth a million such as she, and yet neither he nor you have the sense to see it. I can inform you that Miss Gertrude's arm is sore tonight, but not where you clasped it. She hurt herself more than she injured me when she struck me. Look at this,"—and she drew back her sleeve, disclosing a wrist as pretty as that of Miss Hemster, notwithstanding the fact that one part was both bruised and swollen. "That is where I caught her blow, and can assure you it was given with great force and directness. So, Mr. Tremorne, if you have any sympathy to expend, please let me have the benefit of it, and I will bestow my sympathy upon you in return."

"Indeed, Miss Stretton, I am very sorry to see that you are hurt. I hoped you had warded off the blow slantingly, instead of getting it square on the arm like that."

"Oh, it is nothing," said the girl carelessly, drawing down her sleeve again, "it is merely an exhibit, as they say in the courts, to win the sympathy of a man, and it does n't hurt now in the least, unless I strike it against something. I ask you to believe that I would never have said a word about the girl to you if you had not seen for yourself what those near her have to put up with. You will understand, Mr. Tremorne, I am but a poor benighted woman who has had no one to talk to for months and months. I cannot unburden my soul to Mr. Hemster, because I like him too well; and if I talk to the captain he will merely laugh at me, and tell funny stories. There is no one but you; so you see, unfortunate man, you are the victim of two women."

"I like being the victim of one of them," said I; "but am I to infer from what you have said that, as you don't speak to Mr. Hemster because you like him, you speak to me because you dislike me?"

"What a far-fetched conclusion!" she laughed.

"Certainly not. I like you very much indeed, and even admired you until you used the word 'abjectly' down in that passage. That is a word I detest; no one should employ it when referring to himself."

"Then you *were* in Miss Hemster's room after all."

"I have not said so, and I refuse to admit it. That is hereafter to be a forbidden topic, and a redeemed prisoner in charge of his gaoler must not disobey orders. If it were not for me, you would now be in your room moping and meditating on your wickedness. I have wrestled with you as if I were a Salvation lass, and so you should be grateful."

"Never was a man wallowing in despondency more grateful for the helping hand of a woman enabling him to emerge."

"It is very generous of you to say that, when it was the helping hand of a woman that pushed you into it."

"No, it was my own action that sent me there. I doubt if a man ever gets into the Slough of Despond through the efforts of any one else. A lone man blunders blindly along, and the first thing he knows he is head over ears in the mud,— and serve him right, too."

"Why serve him right?"

"Because he has no business being a lone man. Two heads are better than one; then, if one is making for the ditch, the helping hand of the other restrains."

"Since when did you arrive at so desperate a conclusion, Mr. Tremorne?"

"Since I met you."

"Well, it is a blessing there was no one to restrain you to-day, or otherwise somebody might have been shot. There is something to be said for lack of restraint upon occasion."

"Miss Stretton, if I had had a sensible woman to advise me, I am certain I would never have lost my money."

"Was it a large amount?"

"It was a fortune."

"How one lives and learns! I have often heard that women squander fortunes, but never yet that a woman helped to preserve one."

"It is better for a man's wife to squander a fortune than to allow a stranger to do it."

"Oh, I am not so sure. The end seems to be the same in both cases. I suppose you have in your mind the woman who would have given you good advice at the proper time.

"Yes, I have."

"Then why don't you ask her now, or is it too late?"

"I don't know that she would have anything to do with me; however, it is very easy to find out. Miss Stretton, will you marry me? I have nothing particular to offer you except myself, but I think I 've reached the lowest ebb of my fortunes, and any change must be toward improvement."

"Good gracious, is this actually a proposal?"

"If you will be so generous as to regard it as such."

The young lady stopped in her promenade, and leaned back against the rail, looking me squarely in the face. Then she laughed with greater heartiness than I had yet heard her do.

"This is most interesting," she said at last, "and really most amazing. Why, you must have known me for nearly two hours! I assure you I did not lend you a helping hand out of the Slough of Despond to imprison you at once in the Castle Despair of a penniless marriage. Besides, I always thought a proposal came after a long and somewhat sentimental *camaraderie, which* goes under the name of courtship. However, this explains what I have so often marvelled at in the English papers; a phrase that struck me as strange and unusual: ' A marriage has been arranged and will take place between So-and-So and So-and-So.' Such a proposal as you have just made is surely an arrangement rather than a love affair. Indeed, you have said nothing about love at all, and so probably such a passion does not enter into the amalgamation. If you were not so serious I should have thought you were laughing at me."

"On the contrary, madam, I am very much in earnest, and it is you who are laughing at me."

"Don't you think I 've a very good right to do so? Why, we are hardly even acquainted, and I have no idea what your Christian name is, as I suppose you have no idea what mine is."

"Oh, Hilda, I know your name perfectly!"

"I see you do, and make use of it as well, which certainly advances us another step. But the other half of my proposition is true, and I remain in ignorance of yours."

"When unconsciously I went through the ceremony of christening, I believe my godfathers and godmothers presented me with the name of Rupert."

"What a long time you take in the telling of it. Was n't there a Prince Rupert once? It seems to me I 've heard the phrase 'the Rupert of debate,' and the Rupert of this, and the Rupert of that, so he seems to be a very dashing fellow."

"He was. He dashed into misfortune, as I have often done, but there all likeness between us ends."

"It seems to me the likeness remains, because the present Rupert is dashing into the misfortune of a very heedless proposal. But do not fear that I shall take advantage of your recklessness, which is the more dangerous when you remember my situation. I sometimes think I would almost marry the Prince of Darkness to get out of the position I hold, for I am told he is a gentleman, who probably keeps his temper, and I am coming to the belief that a good temper is a jewel beyond price. However, I 'm exaggerating again. I do not really need to stay here unless I wish it, and I remain for the sake of Mr. Hemster, who, as I told you last night, has always been very kind to me, and for whom I have a great respect and liking. Besides, I am not nearly so helpless as perhaps you may imagine. If I went home I could make a very good living teaching music in the States. So you see I do not need to accept the Prince of Darkness should he offer his hand."

"You mean, *when* he has offered his hand?"

She laughed at this, and went on merrily:

"No, 'if;' not 'when.' I shall always cherish the proposal of Prince Rupert, and when the Prince of Darkness makes advances I shall probably tell him that he is not the first Highness so to honour me. When the sunlight comes to take the place of the moonlight, we shall laugh together over this—I can't call it sentimental episode, shall we term it, business arrangement? Now, would you mind accepting a little advice on the subject of matrimony?"

"I 'll accept your advice if you 'll accept me. Turn about is fair play, you know. Let us finish one transaction before we begin another."

"Transaction is a charming word, Mr. Tremorne, nearly as good as arrangement; I am not sure but it is better. I thought the transaction was finished. You are respectfully declined, with thanks, but, as I assured you, I shall always cherish the memory of this evening, and, now that the way is clear, may I tender this advice, which I have been yearning for some hours to give you. You won't reply. Well, on the whole I think your attitude is very correct. You could hardly be expected to jump joyously from one transaction to another, and I really feel very much flattered that you have put on that dejected look and attitude, which becomes you very much indeed and almost makes me think that the precipitancy of my refusal equals the headlong impetuosity of your avowal. A wiser woman would have asked time for consideration."

"Pray take the time, Miss Stretton; it is not yet too late."

"Yes, it is. What is done, is done, and now comes

117

my advice. You said two heads are better than one. That is true generally, but not always, so I shall present you with an aphorism in place of it, which is that two purses are better than one, if either contains anything. If one purse is always empty, and the other is bursting full, the truth of my adage cannot be questioned. I surmise that your purse and mine are almost on an equality, but I can assure you that Miss Hemster's *portemonnaie* is full to repletion."

" That has nothing to do with me," I answered curtly.

" Oh, but it may have, and much. I noticed when you came down to luncheon yesterday that you are very deeply in love with Miss Hemster."

" My dear Miss Hilda,—I claim the right to call you that,—when one remembers that you never took your eyes from your plate at luncheon I must say that you have most extraordinary powers of observation. You thought I was high and mighty toward Mr. Hemster, which was not the case, and now you assert that I was in love with Miss Hemster, which is equally beside the fact."

" Of course you are bound to say that, and I may add that although I am offering you advice I am not asking confidences in exchange. I assert that you fell in love with Miss Hemster during your charming ramble through Nagasaki; falling in love with a haste which seems to be characteristic of you, and which totally changes the ideas I had previously held regarding an Englishman."

" Yes, a number of your notions concerning the men

of my country were entirely erroneous, as I took the liberty of pointing out to you last night."

"So you did, but actions speak louder than words, and I form my conclusions from your actions. Very well, propose to Miss Hemster; I believe she would accept you, and I further believe that you would prove the salvation of the girl. Her father would make no objection, for I see he already likes you; but in any case he would offer no opposition to anything that his daughter proposed. His life is devoted, poor man, to ministering to her whims and caprices, so you are certain of the parental blessing, and that would carry with it, as I have pointed out, the full purse."

"You spoke of the Prince of Darkness just now, Miss Stretton, so I will appropriate your simile and say that if there were an unmarried Princess of Darkness I would sooner try my luck with her than with Miss Hemster."

"Oh, nonsense! Miss Hemster is a good-hearted girl if only she'd been rightly trained. You would tame her. I know no man so fitted to be the modern Petruchio, and I am fond enough of the drama to say I would like to see a modern rendering of 'The Taming of the Shrew.'"

"She'll never be tamed by me, Miss Stretton."

"She has been, Mr. Tremorne, only you spoiled your lesson by your apology. You must not make a mistake like that again. If you had stood your ground, preserving a distant and haughty demeanour, with a frown on your noble brow, pretty Miss Gertrude would soon have come around to you, wheedling, flattering, and most exquisitely charming, as she well knows how to be. You could then have caught her on the rebound, as the novels put it, just, in fact, as I have managed to catch you to-night. You will be very thankful in the morning that I refused to retain my advantage."

"I shall never be thankful for that, Miss Hilda, and it is equally certain that I shall never propose to Miss Hemster. If I were a speculative adventurer I'd venture to wager on it."

"Most men who see her, propose to her; therefore you must not imagine that Gertrude has not been sought after. I should not be at all certain of your success were it not that every man she has hitherto met has flattered her, while you have merely left the marks of your fingers on her wrists and have threatened to box her ears. This gives you a tremendous advantage if you only know how to use it. I have read somewhere that there is a law in Britain which allows a husband to punish his wife with a stick no bigger than his little finger. I therefore advise you to marry the girl, take something out of the full purse and buy back the ancestral acres, then go into the forest and select a switch as large as the law allows. After that, the new comedy of 'The Taming of the Shrew,' with the married pair living happily ever afterward. You should prove the most fortunate of men, in that you will possess the prettiest, richest, and most docile wife in all your island."

"I am not a barrister, Miss Stretton, therefore can neither affirm nor deny the truth you have stated regarding the law of the stick. If, however, a belief in

that enactment has led you to reject my proposal, I beg
to inform you that I have no ancestral acres containing a forest; therefore I cannot possess myself of a
twig of the requisite size without trespassing on some
one else's timber. So you see you need have no fear on
that score."

" I am not so sure," replied Hilda, shaking her pretty head, " I imagine there must be a Wife-Beaters'
Supply Company in London somewhere, which fur-
nishes the brutal Britisher at lowest rates with the correct legal apparatus for matrimonial correction. I
tremble to think of the scenes that must have been enacted in the numerous strong castles of Britain which
have had new copper roofs put on with the money
brought over by American brides. Girls, obstreperous
and untrained, but wealthy beyond the dreams of avarice, have gone across, scorning the honest straightforward American man, who in my opinion is the most
sincere gentleman of all the world. These rich but
bad-tempered jades have disappeared within the castle,
and the portcullis has come down. Have we ever
heard a whimper from any one of them? Not a whisper even. If they had married American men there
would have been tremendous rows, ending with divorce cases; but not so when they have disappeared
into the castle. You never hear of an American
woman divorcing a lord, and Lord knows some of
those lords are the riff-raff of creation. History gives
us grim pictures of tragical scenes in those old strong-
holds, but I shudder to think of the tragedies which
must occur nowadays when once the drawbridge is up,

and the American girl, hitherto adored, learns the law
regarding flagellation. The punishment must be exceedingly complete, for the lady emerges cowed and
subdued as the Kate that Shakespeare wrote about.
And how well that great man understood a wilful and
tyrannical woman! Oh, you need n't look shocked,
Mr. Tremorne. Have n't you an adage on that benighted island which says 'A woman, a dog, and a
walnut-tree; the more you beat them the better they
be?'"

"Great heavens, girl, what an imagination you
have! You should really write a novel. It would be
an interesting contribution toward international love
affairs."

"I may do so, some day, if music-teaching fails. I
should like, however, to have the confession of one of
the victims of an international matrimonial match."

"Which victim? The English husband or the
American wife?"

"The wife, of course. I think I shall wait until you
and Miss Hemster are married a year or two, and then
perhaps she will look more kindly on me than she does
at present, and so may tell me enough to lend local
colour to my book."

"I can give you a much better plan than that, Miss
Stretton. Hearsay evidence, you know, is never admitted in courts of law, and by the same token it
amounts to very little in books. I am given to understand that, to be successful, an author must have lived
through the events of which he writes, so your best
plan is to accept my offer; then we will purchase a

moated grange in England, and you can depict its horrors from the depths of experience."

"Where are we to get the money for the moated grange? I have n't any, and you 've just acknowledged that you are penniless."

"I forgot that. Still, moated granges are always going cheap. They are damp as a general rule, and not much sought after. We could possibly buy one on the instalment plan, or even rent it if it came to that."

Miss Stretton laughed joyously at the idea, held out her hand, and bade me a cordial good-night.

"Thank you so much, Mr. Tremorne for a most interesting evening, and also for the proposal. I think it very kind of you, for I suppose you suspect I have n't had very many. I think we 've each helped the other out of the Slough of Despond. So good-night, good-night!"

CHAPTER XI

I WAS awakened next morning by the roar of the anchor-chain running out, and found the yacht at a standstill, with the vibration of the machinery temporarily at an end. On looking out through the porthole I recognized the town of Chemulpo, which had grown considerably since I last saw it. Beyond stood the hills of Corea, rising wave upon wave, as if the land had suffered a volcanic eruption.

Mr. Hemster and I had breakfast alone together, after which we went on deck.

" Now," said he, " the captain has brought us safely here without running down an island, and the next move in the game is yours. What do you propose to do? "

" I shall go ashore at once, engage ponies and an escort, change a quantity of silver money into ropes of sek, then I shall make my way as quickly as possible to the capital."

" What are ropes of sek? " asked Mr. Hemster.

" They are bronze, iron, or copper coins, which are strung on ropes of straw by means of a square hole in the middle. They are the most debased currency on earth, and are done up in strings of five hundred cash. Sek is useful in dealing with the natives, but when I come to the capital. I shall need silver and gold. When I have made arrangements at Seoul I shall return to Chemulpo and let you know the result."

"You told me I could not take the ' Michigan ' up the river,—what do you call it,—the Han?—and you were doubtful about the advisability of using the naphtha launch."

" No, the yacht would be sure to run aground before you had gone very far, and as for the naphtha launch, the Han is rather a treacherous and very crooked piece of navigation, and if you had to stop half-way we might be farther from the capital than we are now, with a worse road ahead of us, and no chance of getting ponies or escort. I strongly advise you to stay where you are till I return, and meanwhile I 'll find out more about the river than I know now."

To this Mr. Hemster agreed, and, being well provided with the sinews of war, I went ashore. Chemulpo proved to be quite a commercial town, and there was no difficulty in my getting everything I wanted. I was shocked but not surprised to find that the Prime Minister, whom I formerly knew, and on whose help I had somewhat counted, had been deposed and beheaded, while all his relatives, male and female, had been eliminated from human knowledge by death, slavery, or exile. However, even if this man had remained in office, my best plea with him would have been money, and as I was well provided with this necessity I foresaw no obstacle to my purpose. Having had an early start, and pushing on with more energy than my escort relished, in spite of my promises of recompense, I reached the capital before the great bell rang and the gates were closed.

I had some thought of calling on the British representative, and if I had done so would doubtless have enjoyed better accommodation for the night than fell to my lot; but as, the last time I saw him, I was, like himself, a servant of our Government, I could not bring myself to acknowledge that I was now merely the hired man of an American millionaire, as his daughter had so tersely put it.

Next day I very soon bribed my way to the presence of the then Prime Minister, and was delighted to find in him a certain Hun Woe, whom I had previously known in a very much more subordinate capacity. After our greetings I went straight to the point, and told Hun Woe that I represented a gentleman and his daughter, now at Chemulpo, who wished the honour of a private conference with the Emperor. I also mentioned casually that there was a certain amount of money in this for the Prime Minister if he could bring about the interview. Hun Woe, with many genuflections, informed me that the delight of serving me would more than recompense him for any trouble he was likely to incur, ending his protestations of deep friendship and regard by inquiring how much of the needful the gentleman in Chemulpo would be prepared to place on the table. I replied by naming a sum about one quarter of the amount I was willing to pay. The Prime Minister's eyes glittered, and he made various shrugs of the shoulders and motions with his hands, during the time that he politely intimated to me his rise in the world since last I met him. A cash dividend which would have been ample in those days, he gently hinted, was little less than an insult at the present time. So far as he was himself concerned, he added, his services were freely at my disposal, and none of the silver would stick to *his* fingers; but, as I must be aware, the Court at Seoul was a most grasping and avaricious body, and he should need to disburse freely before my object could be accomplished.

I sighed and shook my head, rising to leave, regretting it was not to be my good fortune to add to the wealth of an old friend, whereupon Hun Woe begged me to be seated again, and, after many declarations of affectionate esteem, was good enough to name a sum which he thought might be sufficient to cover all expenses; and as this came to less than half of what I was willing to dispose of, we speedily reached an agreement. This haggling at the outset was necessary, not only to save Hemster his hardly earned money, but also to satisfy the official that he was driving a shrewd bargain. I accordingly paid the sum in prompt cash to Hun Woe, and then informed him that if everything went off to the satisfaction of my employer a further bonus would be awarded him, depending in size on the celerity and satisfactory nature of the interview. This delighted the honest Premier, and I must admit that he conducted the business with an energy and despatch which was as gratifying as it was unexpected.

East or West, money is a great lubricator, and, as I have said, I was well provided. That very afternoon

Hun Woe secured me an audience with His Imperial Majesty, and for the third or fourth time in my life I stood before the ruler of Corea. I do not know whether he recognized me or not, but it was quite evident that the scent of gold was in the air, and the Emperor did not leave it long in doubt that he intended to acquire as much as might be available of it. By way of introduction, and to show that I was prepared to do the proper thing, I placed a heavy bag of the seductive metal on the shabby deal table before him, begging His Majesty to accept it as an earnest of more to follow. He poured it out on the table, and gloated over it with a miser's eagerness. He had not improved in appearance since last we met. The seams of dissipation had cut deeply into the royal countenance, and his little crinkling pig eyes were even more rapacious and cruel than I remembered them to be.

The proposal to come aboard the yacht was at once dismissed as impracticable. His Majesty would not venture away from his capital, and, above all, he would not risk his precious person on board of anybody's steamship, so, on the whole, it was just as well that Mr. Hemster had not essayed the navigation of the river Han. However, His Majesty was good enough to inform me that although he would not trust his royal person to the care of the infidels, yet he would make up for that by giving so generous a suitor a suite of rooms in the Palace itself, and my principal would therefore have the honour of being the guest of Corea, as one might say. I imagined that this would look as well in the columns of the "New York Herald" as if the Emperor had gone on board the yacht. I fancied that a few lines, something to the following effect, would read very acceptably in the Sunday papers of Chicago, under the head of *Society Notes:*

"Mr. Silas K. Hemster, of this city, and Miss Hemster, occupy a suite of rooms in the royal Palace of Seoul, as guests of the Emperor of Corea."

So, all in all, I was more than satisfied with the speedy and gratifying outcome of my mission to the Corean capital. After retiring from the royal presence I congratulated the Prime Minister upon his method of conducting negotiations and gave him a further payment on account, so that he would not be tempted to falter in well-doing; and as for Hun Woe himself he looked upon me as the most valuable visitor that had set foot in Corea for many years. I distributed backsheesh somewhat indiscriminately among the underlings of the Palace, and early next morning left the royal precincts on my return to Chemulpo, which port I reached without any mishap. Possibly never before in the history of Seoul had business been so rapidly transacted.

I found Mr. Hemster, as usual, sitting on deck in his accustomed chair, as if he had no interest in the negotiations I had been conducting. He listened quietly to my account of the various interviews, and received without comment the bribery bill I presented to him. He did not appear to be so tremendously impressed as I had expected with the royal invitation to visit the Palace, and said he would have preferred to take up his quarters at the chief hotel in the place, but when I told him there was not a hotel in the city fit for a white man to sleep in, he made no demur to the Imperial proposal. It seemed he had visited Chemulpo during my absence, and in consequence of what he heard there he now made some inquiry regarding the safety of a stay in the capital. I told him that as a rule the Coreans were a peaceable people unless incited to violence by the authorities, and as long as we were willing to bribe the authorities sufficiently they would take care that the influx of the newly acquired affluence would not be interfered with. So he asked me to go to Chemulpo and make arrangements for the transport of the party next morning.

I had not seen Miss Hemster on the day I left for Seoul, but she welcomed my return with her former girlish enthusiasm, just as if nothing particular had happened. She seemed to have entirely recovered from her disappointment in not getting to see the Emperor of Japan, and was now effusively enthusiastic over our coming journey. The young woman more than made up for her father's lack of interest in the royal invitation, and I was asked question after question regarding the Palace at Seoul, which I feared would disappoint her when she saw it, because of its dilapidations and general lack of impressiveness. However, a palace was a palace, she averred, and she further pronounced the opinion that the news of their residence there would make Chicago " sit up " when it was cabled over. Miss Stretton sat silent with downcast eyes during this cross-examination, her intelligent face as inscrutable as that of the old millionaire himself. I did not get a word with her that evening, and, as it was drawing late, I had to return to Chemulpo to make arrangements for the trip the following day, and so stayed ashore that night.

We had a beautiful day for our expedition, and rather a jolly trip of it,— almost, as Miss Hemster said, as if it were a picnic. At Miss Hemster's request I rode by her side, with Miss Stretton sometimes with us, but more often in front, with the old gentleman, who jogged moodily on, absorbed in his own meditations, saying nothing to anybody. Miss Hemster chatted very gaily most of the day, but as evening drew on she became tired of talk and began to look anxiously for the gate of Seoul. When at last we passed through it she expressed great contempt for the city of shanties, as she called it, giving somewhat petulant expression to her disgust at the disillusionment for which I had unsuccessfully endeavoured to prepare her. Of course by the time we reached the Palace the ladies were tired out, and, if we had had the slightest notion of what was before us, anxiety would have been added to fatigue.

CHAPTER XII

WE were more comfortable in the royal apartments than might have been expected. Mr. Hemster had brought his own cook with him, together with the Japanese boy to wait on us, and he had also taken the precaution to bring a week's provisions, so that in spite of the primitive arrangements of the kitchen placed at our disposal we fared very much as usual so far as the cuisine was concerned. The officials made no complaint at this reflection on their hospitality; in fact, they rather relished our foresight, because, as Hun Woe admitted with great simplicity, it enabled them to charge our keep to the royal exchequer and yet incur no expense in providing for us. A system which admits of collection and no disbursements is heavenly to a Corean official. We were probably at the outset the most popular party that had ever lodged in the royal Palace.

Our first dilemma arose, not through any interference from the officers of the Court, but because of certain objections which Miss Gertrude Hemster herself promulgated. The Prime Minister did us great honour in offering to coach us personally regarding the etiquette that surrounds the approach to the throne. It seemed that both Emperor and Empress were to receive us in state, and the moment we came in sight of their Majesties we were to turn our faces aside, as if dazzled by the magnificence before us and the glory conferred upon us march a dozen steps to the left, turn again, march a dozen steps to the right, bowing extremely low at each evolution, advancing, with great caution and humility, never more than two steps forward at a time, approaching the throne by a series of crab-like movements and coming very gradually forward, zigzag fashion, until we stood with heads humbly inclined before the two potentates. My translation of all this caused great hilarity on the part of Miss Hemster, and she quite shocked the genial Prime Minister by giving way to peal after peal of laughter. After all, he was a dignified man and did not regard the ceremony as a joke, which appeared to be the way it presented itself to the young lady.

" I 'm not going through any of that nonsense," she exclaimed. " Does he think I intend to make a Wild West show of myself? If he does, he 's mistaken. I 'll proceed right up to the Emperor and shake hands with him, and if he does n't like it he can lump it. You translate that to him, Mr. Tremorne."

I intimated respectfully to the young woman that Court etiquette was Court etiquette, and that everything would be much more simple if we fell in with the ways of the country. This marching and countermarching was no more absurd than our own way of shaking hands, or the Pacific Island method of salutation by rubbing noses.

" ' When in Rome do as the Romans do,' " I suggested; but this expostulation had no effect whatever upon the determined young person, who became more and more set in her own way from the fact that her father quietly agreed with me. Furthermore, when she learned that there were no chairs in the Royal reception-room, she proclaimed that her Japanese attendant must carry a chair for her; because, if the Royal pair were seated, she insisted on being seated also. I was to tell " His Nibs,"—by which expression she referred to the smiling Prime Minister,—that she belonged to sovereign America, and therefore was as much an Empress in her own right as the feminine Majesty of Corea.

"Miss Hemster," said I, "I don't know whether what you wish can be accomplished or not; but in any case it is sure to cause considerable delay, and, furthermore, it will probably cost your father a very large sum of money."

I speedily saw that I would better have preserved silence. The young lady drew herself up with great dignity and flashed upon me a glance of withering indignation.

"Will you oblige me by minding your own business?" she asked harshly. "Your duty is to obey orders, and not to question them."

To this, of course, no reply was possible, so I contented myself by bowing to her, and, turning to Hun Woe, who stood smiling first at one and then at the other of us, not understanding even the drift of our conversation, but evidently growing somewhat uneasy at the tone it was taking, I translated to him as well as

I could what Miss Hemster had said, softening the terms as much as possible, and laying great stress on her exalted position in her own country, of which land the Prime Minister was enormously ignorant.

Hun Woe became extremely grave; and his smile, unlike that in the advertisement, at once " came off."

" If the strenuous Empress of China," said I, " arrived at Seoul on a visit, she would certainly be received by His Majesty as an equal, and would not need to go through the ceremony of advance which you have so graphically described. Now this Princess," I continued, " holds herself to be of a rank superior to the Empress of China, and is considered of higher status by her own countrymen."

The Prime Minister very solemnly shook his head and seemed much disquieted.

" Her father," I continued earnestly, and in a measure truthfully, " maintains a much larger fleet than China possesses, and his private war-ship, now in the waters of Corea, is grander than anything that empire ever beheld, much less owned. His territories are vast. Thousands of people,— yes, millions,— pay tribute to him. He has waged commercial war against those who dared to dispute his authority, and has invariably defeated them. His revenue exceeds that of the kingdom of Corea twice over, so is it likely,—I put it to you as man to man,—that such a potentate will consent to the dozen steps this way, and the dozen steps that? His only daughter is the Crown Princess, and will be heiress to all his powers and emoluments. I pray you, therefore, put this matter in its right light before His Majesty of Corea, and I can assure you, if you succeed, your own income will be largely augmented."

This speech undoubtedly impressed the Premier, who bowed low to Mr. Hemster and his daughter time and again as I went on. The girl's anger had subsided as quickly as it had risen, and she watched us both intently, seeming at first to doubt that I translated accurately what I had been so curtly ordered to say; but as our conversation went on the increasing deference of the Prime Minister showed that I was at least doing my best. The old gentleman, too, regarded us shrewdly from under his bushy eyebrows, but seemed rather tired of the game, as if it were not worth such a pow-wow. He evidently wished to get the whole thing over as quickly as possible, and return to the comforts of his yacht, and in this I entirely sympathized with him.

The Prime Minister replied that he would present the new facts before His Majesty, and averred that if they had the same effect upon the Emperor of Corea as they had produced upon the Prime Minister the impediment would be speedily removed. He assured me I could count on his utmost endeavours to find a solution for the unexpected exigency, and I was well aware that my tale would not decrease in the retelling. With many and most profound obeisances to the two Western grandees, the Prime Minister took his departure, and I accompanied him outside, where I made him a payment on a gold basis.

The Royal audience had been appointed for two o'clock of the afternoon on the day succeeding our arrival at Seoul, but this new question that had arisen caused the ceremony to be postponed, much to my annoyance, for I knew the habitual delay of these people, especially where money was in question, and I feared that the inconvenient assumption of dignity on the part of the young woman might land us in trouble of which neither she nor her father had the least appreciation. I communicated my fears of delay and complications to the old gentleman when I got him alone, hoping he might use his influence with his daughter to modify what seemed to me her ill-timed assertion of high rank; but Mr. Hemster, though a resourceful man in every other direction, always proved a broken reed so far as his daughter was concerned, and he pathetically admitted his inability to curb either her actions or her words.

"All we can do, Mr. Tremorne," he said, "is to fork over the cash. Don't you spare it. I can see very well you are handling this situation as expertly as a ward politician. You 're all right. If you can talk to this here King as you talked to his Prime Minister, I think you 'll fix up the thing in five minutes, and remember this is a game of bluff in which there is no limit. I don't restrict you in the cash you spend, so go ahead."

And this indeed proved to be the way out of the muddle, although I explained to him that too lavish distribution of cash was not without its own danger. But at this juncture a message arrived to the effect that the Prime Minister wished to see me, and I at once departed to learn what had been the outcome of his mediation. I found that he had made little progress, but by a curious coincidence he put forth the same suggestion previously offered by Mr. Hemster. He had arranged a conference for me with the King, and advised me, as Mr. Hemster had done, to lay it on thick. Hun Woe was somewhat encouraged by the orders he had received from his royal master in regard to my audience. The King would receive me entirely alone; not even his Prime Minister was to be present. From this condition Hun Woe surmised I was to be successful in my quest, and I was well aware that this unwitnessed reception of me was as much contrary to Corean customs as was the proposal Miss Hemster had made.

I saw his Majesty in one of the private apartments of the Palace, and speedily realized that he did not care a rap what honours belonged to Mr. Hemster. The sinister, shifty eyes of his Majesty were filled with greed. Never was there such a picture of avarice presented to me as the countenance of the King showed. His claw-like hands had been withdrawn from the voluminous bell sleeves of his robe of red silk and yellow gold, and were twitching nervously on the table before him. His tremulous attitude of uneasy eagerness reminded me of the Miser in the " Chimes of Normandy." Impatiently he waved aside the recital touching the claims of my employer to the most-favoured-monarch treatment, and gasped out the Corean equivalent for " How much, how much ? "

A tangible object-lesson is better than talk even in the Orient; so, bringing my eloquence to an abrupt conclusion, I drew from my pocket another bag of gold, similar in weight to the one I had previously presented to him, and, seeing he was impatient for touch as well as for sight, undid the string and poured the stream of shining metal discs before him on the table. He thrust his vibrant hands among the coins, and gave utterance to a low guttural sound of satisfaction which resembled the noise made by a pig thrusting its snout into a trough of slops, rather than any exclamation I had ever before heard from human lips. I assured him that no word of all this would be spoken by me, and promised that as soon as the conference was safely over on the terms that Miss Hemster and her father had laid down, a similar amount would be privately paid to his Royal self in an equally secret manner; and so my mission terminated in a glorious success, and it was arranged that the reception should take place the next day at two o'clock. The process was costly, but effective; and effectiveness, after all, was the main thing.

I reported my victory to Mr. Hemster and his daughter, and almost immediately after this the Prime Minister came in to offer his congratulations. The good man had seen his royal master for a few moments, and was evidently delighted that everything was going on so smoothly. It meant money in his pocket, and he was becoming rich with a celerity which left stock-exchange speculations far in the rear. He had received his commands regarding next day's reception, and the Emperor had been pleased to order that the audience should take place in the same room where I had seen him, with none of the nobles of the Court present except the Prime Minister. This was a good example of his Majesty's craftiness. The Premier already knew that the etiquette of the Court was to be put aside for the occasion; but the monarch had no desire for further witnesses, and was evidently not going to set a precedent in the realm of Corea that might produce inconvenient consequences thereafter.

I had had little opportunity of talking with Miss Stretton since the night of our walk on deck,—the night of the proposal, as I called it to myself, as amidst all these negotiations I kept continually thinking of it. Without exactly avoiding me, Miss Stretton never seemed to be alone, and although very rarely I caught a glance of her eye I had no opportunity of private speech with her. She kept very much in the background and was more than usually quiet and thoughtful.

We had dinner early that night, somewhere about six o'clock, for there were neither candles nor lamps in the Palace, and if we waited until nightfall we had to " grope," as Mr. Hemster termed it. In spite of the success of her plans, Miss Hemster was distinctly snappy at dinner, if I may use such a term regarding a person so beautiful. She shut me up most effectually when I ventured a little harmless general conversation, and I think she made Miss Stretton feel more than usual the bitterness of a dependent's bread. Mr. Hemster said nothing. I could see the poor old gentleman was hankering for a daily paper, and from my soul I felt sorry for him as he listened with the utmost patience to the querulous fault-findings of his lovely daughter.

Toward the end of dinner something that was said did not please the young lady, and she rose abruptly and left the table, with a gesture of queenly disapproval of us all. Anger appeared to fill her as electricity fills an accumulator, and until the battery was discharged we never knew who would suffer the next shock. When the young woman's ill-temper had been aroused by my opposition earlier in the day, perhaps we would have spent a pleasanter evening if it had been allowed to run its course. But as it was checked by her interest in the negotiations it now filtered out in very palpable discontent. When Miss Stretton arose to leave I took the liberty of begging her to remain.

" I should like very much," I said, " to show you the light on Nam-san."

" And what is the light on Nam-san? " she asked, pausing with her hand on the back of the chair.

" Beacons are lighted all along the coast of Corea, on the mountain tops," I replied, " so that peak calls to peak, as it were; and the last one to be lit is that on Nam-san, which is the name of the highest mountain near Seoul. They kindle it at eight o'clock, and its blazing up shows that the kingdom of Corea is safe and at peace with the world."

" Very well," said Miss Stretton after a pause; " I will return here about ten minutes to eight."

She was as good as her word, and we took a stroll together in the great courtyard of the Palace, which is a city within a city. The gates of the Palace grounds were now closed and guarded, and we could not have got out into Seoul if we had wished to do so. But it was all very still and pleasant in the broad square surrounded by the low, strangely roofed buildings that constituted the Palace. We saw the beacon light flash out and then die away. I cannot remember that we talked much, but there was a calm and soothing sense of comradeship between us that was very comforting. She told me, when I had tried to warn her against expecting too much on seeing the Emperor next day, that she did not intend to accompany our party, and I suspected that she had been ordered to remain away. Moreover I could see that she was very tired of it all, and, like Mr. Hemster, wished herself back in her own country.

CHAPTER XIII

SHORTLY before two o'clock the next day the Prime Minister came for us, and conducted us directly to the Presence Chamber, instead of taking us to the small wooden building, containing a table and some chairs, where visitors usually had to wait until the Emperor's messenger arrived with orders permitting an advance to the throne-room. Our little procession consisted of four persons,—Mr. Hemster, Miss Hemster, the Prime Minister, and myself. Hun Woe was visibly uneasy, and I was well aware that, in spite of the money paid him, he would much rather have been absent from the ceremony. In Eastern lands it is extremely dangerous for a Vizier to witness a Sultan's humiliation, and the Prime Minister well knew that although the Emperor had permitted the deference due to him to be temporarily annulled through payment of gold, he might nevertheless consider it desirable to eliminate the onlooker, so that no record of this innovation were left on the earth.

The room into which we were conducted was but indifferently lighted. It was oblong in shape, and a low divan ran across the farther end of it. Four very ordinary wooden chairs had been placed midway between the door and the divan.

Both the Emperor and the Empress were seated, Oriental fashion, on huge cushions, and were decked out in a fashion that might be termed tawdry gorgeousness. I do not know whether the strings of colored gems that hung around the Empress were real or imitation, but they were barbaric in size and glitter and number. The Empress, whom I had never seen before, sat impassive, with eyes half closed, as if she were a statue of the feminine Buddha. During the whole of the exciting interview she never moved or showed the slightest sign of animation.

The Emperor's ferret-like eyes glanced shiftily over the advancing party, which came forward, as I might say, in two sections, the three white people upright, and the Premier bending almost double, working his way toward the divan by zigzag courses, giving one the odd notion that he was some sort of wild beast about to spring upon the Emperor when he arrived at a proper position for the pounce.

The twinkling eyes of the Emperor, however, speedily deserted the rest of our party, and fixed themselves on Miss Hemster, who moved toward him with graceful ease and an entire absence of either fear or deference. She instantly made good the determination she had previously expressed, and, gliding directly up to him, thrust forward her hand, which the Emperor seemed at a loss what to do with. His eyes were fastened on her lovely countenance, and there broke on his lips a smile so grim and ghastly that it might well have made any one shudder who witnessed it. The bending Prime Minister uttered a few words which informed the Emperor that the lady wished to shake hands with him, and then his Majesty took his own grimy paws from out of the great bell sleeves in which they were concealed, and with his two hands grasped hers. Never did so sweet a hand disappear in so revolting a clutch, and the young woman, evidently shocked at the contact, and doubtless repelled by the repulsiveness of the face that leered up at her, drew suddenly back, but the clutch was not relaxed.

"Let me go!" she cried breathlessly, and her father took an impulsive step forward; but before he reached her the Emperor suddenly put forth his strength and drew the young woman tumbling down to the divan beside him, grimacing like a fiend from the bottomless pit. Little he recked what he was doing. With a scream Miss Hemster sprang up, flung out her right arm, and caught him a slap on the side of his face that sounded through the hall like the report of a pistol. The Prime Minister, with a shuddering cry of horror, flung himself on his face, and grovelled there in piteous pretence of not having seen this death-earning insult which the Western woman had so energetically bestowed on the Eastern potentate. Hun Woe's open palms beat helplessly against the wooden planks, as if he were in the tremors of dissolution. The active young woman sprang back a pace or two, and, if a glance could have killed, the look with which she transfixed his Imperial Majesty would have brought extinction with it.

As for the Emperor, he sat there, bending slightly forward, the revolting grimace frozen on his face, and

yet his royal head must have been ringing with the
blow he had received. The Empress sat stolid, as if
nothing had happened, and never moved an eyelid.
Then his Majesty, casting a look of contempt at the
huddled heap of clothes which represented the Prime
Minister, threw back his head and gave utterance to a
cackling laugh which was exceedingly chilling and unpleasant to hear. Meanwhile the young lady seated
herself emphatically in one of the chairs, with a sniff
of indignant remonstrance.

"There," she said, "I flatter myself I have taught
one nigger a lesson in good manners. He'll bear the
signature of my fingers on his cheeks for a few hours
at least."

"Madam," I said solemnly, "I beg you to restrain
yourself. Your signature is more likely to prove a
death-warrant than a lesson in etiquette."

"Be quiet," she cried angrily to me, turning toward
me a face red with resentment; "if there is no one
here to protect me from insult I must stand up for myself, and you can bet your bottom dollar I'll do it. Do
you think I am afraid of an old hobo like that?"

The Emperor watched her with narrowing eyes as
she was speaking, and it really seemed as if he understood what she said; for again he threw back his head
and laughed, as if the whole thing was a joke.

"Madam," said I, "it isn't a question of fear or the
lack of it, but merely a matter of common sense. We
are entirely in this man's power."

"He dare n't hurt us," she interrupted with a snap,
"and he knows it, and you know it."

"I beg your pardon, Miss Hemster, I know a great deal more of these people than you do. No Westerner can predict what may happen in an Eastern Court."

"Westerners are just as good as New Yorkers, or Londoners either, for that matter," cried the gentle Gertrude, holding her head high in the air.

"You mistake me, Miss Hemster; I am speaking of Europeans as well as of Americans. This Emperor, at a word, can have our heads chopped off before we leave the room."

"Oh, you 're a finicky, babbling old woman," she exclaimed, tossing her head, "and just trying to frighten my father. The Emperor knows very well that if he laid a hand on us the United States would smash his old kingdom in two weeks."

"If you will pardon me, madam, the Emperor is quite ignorant. If he should determine to have us executed, not all the United States or Britain and Europe combined could save us. He has but to give an order, and it will be rigidly obeyed if the heavens fell the moment after. If you are anxious to give the Emperor your opinion of him, all I beg of you is that you wait until we 're out of this trap, and then send it to him on a picture post-card. Whatever action the Powers might subsequently take would be of no assistance to us—when we are executed."

During this heated conversation the Prime Minister had partly risen to his hands and knees, although he kept his head hanging down until it nearly touched the floor. The Emperor had been watching Miss Hemster's animated countenance, and he seemed greatly to enjoy my evident discomfiture. Even though he understood no word of our language, he saw plainly enough that I was getting the worst of the verbal encounter. Now the gradual uprising of the Prime Minister drew his attention temporarily to this grovelling individual, and he spoke a few words to him which at once raised my alarm for the safety of those in my care. His Majesty had evidently forgotten for the moment that I understood the Corean tongue. Hun Woe now rose to his feet, kept his back at an angle of forty-five degrees, and, without turning around, began to retreat from the Imperial presence. I at once stepped in his way, and said to the Emperor that this command must not go forth, whereupon the Majesty of Corea was good enough to laugh once more.

"What are you talking about?" demanded Miss Hemster. "You must translate everything that is said; and, furthermore, you must tell him that he has to apologize to me for his insult at the beginning."

"All in good time, Miss Hemster."

"Not all in good time," she cried, rising from her chair. "If you don't do that at once, I'll go and slap his face again."

"Please believe me, Miss Hemster, that you have already done that once too often. I assure you that the situation is serious, and you are increasing the danger by your untimely interference."

Before she could reply, a roar of laughter from the Emperor, who wagged his head from side to side and rocked his body to and fro in his glee, drew my attention to the fact that I had been outwitted. The Prime

Minister, taking advantage of my discussion with Miss Hemster, had scuttled silently away and had disappeared. I fear I made use of an exclamation to which I should not have given utterance in the presence of a lady; but that lady's curiosity, overcoming whatever resentment she may have felt, clamoured to know what had happened.

"His Majesty," said I, "gave orders to the Prime Minister doubly to guard the Palace gates, and see that no communication reached the outside from us. It means that we are prisoners!"

All this time I had not the least assistance from the old gentleman, who sat in a most dejected attitude on one of the wooden chairs. I had remained standing since we entered the room. Now he looked up with dismay on his countenance, and I was well enough acquainted with him to know that his fear was not for himself but for his daughter.

"Will you tell the Emperor," he said, "that we are armed, and that we demand leave to quit this place as freely as we entered it?"

"I think, Mr. Hemster," said I, "that we had better conceal the fact that we have arms,— at least until the Prime Minister returns. We can keep that as our trump card."

"Will you please do exactly what my father tells you to," snapped the young woman sharply.

"Hush, Gertrude!" said Mr. Hemster. Then, addressing himself to me: "Sir," he added, "do whatever you think is best."

I now turned to the Emperor, and made the speech

of my life. I began by stating that Corea had been
face to face with many a crisis during its history, but
never had she been confronted with such a situation as
now presented itself. Mr. Hemster, besides being
King, in his own right, of the provision market in Chicago, was one of the most valued citizens of the United
States, and that formidable country would spend its last
sen and send its last man to avenge any injury done
to Mr. Hemster, or the Princess, his daughter. I asserted that the United States was infinitely more pow-
erful than Russia, China, and Japan added together,
with each of whom he had hitherto chiefly dealt. This
alone would be bad enough, but the danger of the situation was augmented by my own presence. His Majesty might perhaps be good enough to remember that
the last time I had had the pleasure of meeting him I
was an Envoy of a country which had probably fought
more successful battles than any other nation in existence. Great Britain was also in the habit of avenging
the injuries inflicted on her subjects; and so, if the
Emperor was so ill-fated as to incur the displeasure
of these mighty empires, whose united strength was
sufficient to overawe all the rest of the earth, he would
thus bring about the extinction of himself and of his
nation.

I regret to say that this eloquence was largely thrown
away. His Majesty paid but scanty attention to my
international exposition. His fishy eyes were fixed
continually on Miss Hemster, who now and then made
grimaces at him as if she were a little schoolgirl, once
going so far as to thrust out her tongue, which action

seemed to strike the Emperor as exceedingly comic, for he laughed uproariously at it.

When I had ceased speaking the Emperor replied in a few words, but without ever taking his eyes from the girl. I answered him,—or, rather, was answering him,—when Miss Hemster interrupted impatiently:

"What are you saying? You must translate as you go on. I wish you would remember your position, Mr. Tremorne, which is that of translator. I refuse to be kept in the dark in this way."

"Gertie, Gertie!" remonstrated her father. "Please do not interfere. Mr. Tremorne will tell us what is happening all in good time."

And now the Emperor himself, as if he understood what was being said, commanded me to translate to them the terms he had laid down.

"I shall try to remember my position, Miss Hemster," I replied; "and, as his Majesty's ideas coincide with your own, I have pleasure in giving you a synopsis of what has passed."

Then I related my opening speech to the Emperor, which appeared to commend itself to Mr. Hemster, who nodded several times in support of my dissertation on the national crisis.

"The Emperor," I continued, "has made no comment upon what I have laid before him. He tells us we are free to go,—that is, your father and myself,—as long as we leave you here. Not to put too fine a point to it, he offers to buy you, and says he will make you the White Star of his harem, which he seems to think is rather a poetical expression."

"Well, of all the gall!" exclaimed Miss Hemster, raising her hands and letting them fall helplessly into her lap again, as if this gesture should define the situation better than any words she had at her command. "You inform His Nibs that I am no White Star Line, and you tell this mahogany graven image that my father can buy him and his one-horse kingdom and give them away without ever feeling it. When he talks of buying, just inform him that in the States down South we used to sell better niggers than him every day in the week."

I thought it better to tone down this message somewhat, and in doing so was the innocent cause, as I suspect, of a disaster which has always troubled my mind since that eventful time. I said to the Emperor that American customs differed from those of Corea. Miss Hemster, being a Princess in her own rank, of vast wealth, could not accept any position short of that of Empress, and, as there was already an Empress of Corea, the union he proposed was impossible. I reiterated my request that we be allowed to pass down to the coast without further molestation.

This statement was received by the Emperor with much hilarity. He looked upon it merely as an effort on my part to enhance the price of the girl, and expressed his willingness to turn over to her half the revenues of the kingdom. He seemed to imagine he was acting in the most lavishly generous manner, and I realized the hopelessness of the discussion, because I was face to face with a man who had never been refused anything he wished for since he came to the throne. His conceited ignorance regarding the power of other countries to enforce their demands made the situation all the more desperate.

At this juncture the crouching Prime Minister returned, made his way slowly, by means of acute angles, to the foot of the throne, and informed the Emperor that the guards of the Palace had been doubled, and had received instructions to allow no living thing to enter or leave the precincts of the Court. I now repeated to Hun Woe the warning I had so fruitlessly proffered to the Emperor, but I doubt if the satellite paid much more attention than his master had done. While in the presence he seemed incapable of either thought or action that did not relate to his Imperial chief. He intimated that the audience was now finished and done with, and added that he would have the pleasure of accompanying us to our rooms. It seemed strange, when we returned, to find Miss Stretton sitting in a chair, placidly reading a book which she had brought with her from the yacht, and the Japanese boy setting out cups for tea on a small table near her. Miss Stretton looked up pleasantly as we entered, closing her book, and putting her finger in it to mark the place.

"What a long time you have been," she said; "the conference must have proved very successful."

Miss Gertrude Hemster paced up and down the room as if energetic action were necessary to calm the perturbation of her spirit. As the other finished her remark she clenched her little fist and cried:

153

" I 'll make that Emperor sit up before I 've done with him ! "

I thought it more advisable to refrain from threats until we were out of the tiger's den; but the reticent example of Mr. Hemster was upon me, and I said nothing. Nevertheless the young woman was as good as her word.

CHAPTER XIV

THE Hemsters had fallen into the English habit of afternoon tea, and, having finished the refreshing cup, I excused myself and went outside to learn how strict the cordon around us was kept. I found that the Prime Minister had done his work well. The gates were very thoroughly guarded, and short of force there seemed to be no method of penetrating into the city. I tried bribery, desiring to get a short note through to the British Consul-General, and, although my bribe was willingly accepted, I found later that the missive was never sent.

Rambling around the vast precincts of the Palace, trying to discover any loophole of escape, I came upon our escort and the ponies which had brought us from the port to the capital. These had been gathered up in the city and taken inside. I could not decide at the moment whether this move on the part of our gaolers strengthened or weakened our position. The escort was composed of a very poor set of creatures who would prove utterly valueless if the crisis developed into a contest. They were all huddled together under a shed, and were very evidently in a state of hopeless panic. They knew intuitively that things were going badly with us, and it needed no prophet to foretell that they would instantly betray us if they got the chance, or cut our throats if they were ordered to do so. I deeply regretted now that we had not stayed longer at Chemulpo until we had gathered together an escort composed entirely of Japanese. Two Japanese followers were among our crowd, and they now stood apart with the imperturbable nonchalance of their race. I was aware that I could depend upon them to the death; but the rest were the very scum of the East, cowardly, unstable as water, and as treacherous as quicksand. I spoke a few words of encouragement to the Japanese, patted the ponies, and then returned to Mr. Hemster. I told him I had endeavoured to send a note to the British representative in Seoul, and to my amazement found that he did not approve of this move.

"The fact is, Mr. Tremorne, we have acted like a parcel of fools, and if this thing ever gets out we shall be the laughing-stock of the world. I don't want either the American or the British Consul to know anything of our position. God helps those who help themselves. I don't want to boast at all, but I may tell you I 'm a dead shot with a revolver, and I have one of the best here with me, together with plenty of cartridges. This expertness with a gun is a relic of my old cowboy days on the plains, and if these here Coreans attempt to interfere with me, somebody is going to get hurt. You have another revolver, and if you are any good with it I guess we 'll have no difficulty in forcing our way through this flock of sheep. Have you learned whether your two Japanese can shoot or not? If they can, I 've got revolvers here for them, and it seems to me that four of us can put up a bluff that will carry us through this tight place. If it was n't that we have women with us, I would n't mind the encounter in the least. As it is, we 'll have to do the best we can, and I propose that we start to-morrow as soon as the gates are opened."

" All right, Mr. Hemster, I believe your diagnosis of the case is correct. I can trust the Japanese, and I think I may say you can trust me."

A little later in the day, the Prime Minister, accompanied by an imposing following, came to me, and with much circumlocution made formal proposal of marriage to Miss Hemster on behalf of the Emperor of Corea. The misguided man appeared to think that this smoothed away all difficulty, and that the only question now to be settled was the amount of money the honoured lady's father would pay down as dowry. Hun Woe fatuously ventured to hope that it would be large in proportion to the elevation in station which awaited the young lady. I replied that Mr. Hemster considered himself equal in rank, and greatly superior in wealth and power, to the Emperor of Corea; that he was now practically held prisoner in the Palace; therefore, if negotiations were to continue, he must be set free, and allowed to return to his own battleship, in which I should be happy to carry on the discussion in a manner which I hoped would prove satisfactory to all parties concerned.

The Prime Minister replied that what I proposed was impossible. The Emperor was completely infatuated with Miss Hemster, and only as a great concession,—due, Hun Woe said, to his own pleadings, which he hoped would be remembered when settlements were made,—did his Majesty consent to a marriage. The Prime Minister continued with many professions of friendship for myself, urging me therefore, as he pretended to have urged the Emperor, to put myself in a reasonable frame of mind. He had never known the Emperor so determined in any course of action before, and lack of compliance on the part of our company would do no good, and might lead to irretrievable disaster. The Emperor had resolved, if his offer were refused, to seize the young lady, and to behead her father, myself, and the whole party who accompanied her. He therefore trusted humbly that I would not thwart his efforts toward an amicable understanding.

I said he must surely have mistaken his instructions; the barbarous programme he had proposed would shock the civilized world. He answered, with a shrug of his shoulders, that the civilized world would never hear of it. I averred he was mistaken in this, telling him I had already communicated with my Consul, and his reply to this was to pull from his sleeve the hasty note I had written and bribed the man at the gate to deliver. This man, he said, had at once brought the communication to him, and he hoped I would acknowledge the fruitlessness of further opposition.

I quickly saw that we were in a predicament, and that it would need all my diplomacy to find a means of egress. However, I determined first to impress upon Hun Woe the dangers of the plan he had outlined. If the Emperor did what he proposed to do, that would bring upon Corea the irretrievable disaster of invasion by both the United States and England. It was not possible to keep assassinations secret. Mr. Hemster's great steamship was at this moment awaiting him at Chemulpo. If no one returned, the captain of that boat had orders to communicate at once with both the British and the American authorities. I endeavored to flatter Hun Wee by telling him that an official of his great learning and intelligence must realize what the result would be. The good man sighed, but in the presence of his *entourage* apparently had not the courage to admit that Corea would come badly out of the encounter. In fact, he said that the Emperor could defend his country against the combined forces of the world; but whether he believed this or not, I should hesitate to say.

I now changed my tactics, and told the Prime Minister that I was merely Ambassador for Mr. Hemster, and that I would inform him of the offer the Emperor had made. It was more than likely, I asserted, that the proposal would be extremely gratifying to him; so we would postpone further consideration until he had time to think over the matter. I further suggested that we should have another interview with the Emperor at the same hour next day, and with this the Prime Minister joyously concurred. To assist the negotiations he told me that the Emperor had referred to my objection of an existing Empress, but means would be found to divorce that august lady, and this he wished me to place before Mr. Hemster and his daughter. He seemed to imagine that thus had been removed the last obstacle to the proposed union, and I said I would put all this in the most favourable light before Mr. Hemster. The conference which had begun so tempestuously therefore ended in a calm that was extremely gratifying to the Prime Minister, who quite evidently hoped that everybody would be reasonable, that the flow of gold should not cease, and that the contest might end happily. So, with many gestures and expressions of deep regard for myself and my companions, the distinguished party withdrew.

I was anxious to see Mr. Hemster alone, so that I might communicate to him the result of my interview with the Prime Minister, but this intention was frustrated. Gertrude Hemster had nothing whatever to occupy her mind, and the adage informs us that mischief is provided for all such persons. She was already aware that this gorgeous deputation had waited upon me, and it required all her father's persuasion to keep her from breaking in upon us and learning what was going on. The curiosity of woman has before now wrecked many promising undertakings, and this threatened to be the fate of Mr. Hemster's plan. The young lady was frank enough to say that she believed me to be playing a double game; not interpreting correctly the message of the Emperor or the sayings of the Prime Minister. She refused to incur the risk of a forced exit from the Palace, and was sure that if the Emperor was rightly spoken to we would all be allowed to march to the port with a royal escort and the honours of war. She insisted that if I were not a coward I would myself brave the dangers of the exit, go to the American Consulate, and there get an interpreter who would be official, and also bring the Consul himself. She was not going to be frightened out of Seoul by a mud-colored heathen like the Emperor, and if only we had treated him as she had done, there would have been no trouble.

I must admit that I agreed with the girl so far as calling in the aid of the American Consul was concerned, and I told her I was quite willing to force the gate and make a run for it to the little spot of the United States which existed in Seoul. But her father could be a determined man when he liked, and this time he put down his foot, declaring firmly that he would not have the news of this fiasco get abroad if he could help it. Curiously enough, Mr. Hemster seemed to have more fear of the yellow press of America than of the yellow man of Corea. His daughter, however, feared neither, and seemed in fact to relish the publicity which this episode might give to her. Whether it was bravery or recklessness on her part, I could not get her to see that we were in any serious danger; but this did not matter, for on appeal to her father to postpone the proposed exodus he proved adamant, and for once the young lady was forced to acquiesce.

I took the pair of extra pistols, and, with ample ammunition, sought out the two Japanese members of our party. I found that both of them had served in the Japanese army and were quite capable of handling firearms with effect. I then told them to say nothing to their Corean comrades, but, as soon as the gates were open in the morning, to bring ponies for the whole party to our door. The manner in which they carried out this order showed their alertness to the exigencies of the situation.

When we all emerged in the morning,— we four white people, our Chinese cook and Japanese serving-boy,—ten ponies were at our door, two of them being loaded down with heavy strings of cash which we had not found occasion to use, because our dealings had been entirely with higher classes and so we had had to employ silver and gold. But only one Japanese man was there. When I asked him where the other fellow was, he replied he was holding a revolver over the huddled heap of Coreans so that they would not give the alarm. As soon as we were mounted, he said he would call his comrade, who would instantly respond.

This proved a very wise precaution, and gave us some valuable minutes before the Palace was roused. We had arrived at the gates ere the sleepy guards realized what was upon them, and the first warning the Palace received of our attempt was the wild firing of the useless muskets which the guards possessed. We had determined not to shoot, hoping that the guards would give way when they found we were resolved to emerge; but their reckless firing, which luckily did no harm to any of our party, made any further attempt at silence unnecessary, and lucky it was for us that we were free to fire, because Mr. Hemster whipped out his revolver at once and shattered the hand of a man who attempted to close the gates. This wounded creature set up such a howl that the guards immediately threw down their arms and fled, leaving the way clear before us.

Now we were in the main street of Seoul, and if it had not been for Mr. Hemster's prohibition I would strongly have advised making directly for the Consulate of either one nation or the other. However, his orders were to press on to the western gate before the alarm should extend through the city. This we did. Now that we were clear of the royal gates, the guards seemed to have resumed their firearms and were evidently determined to make the Emperor believe that they had been extremely valorous, for a regular fusillade greeted our departure down the main street of Seoul. Whatever commotion the firing may have aroused in the Palace, it certainly had an extraordinary effect upon the city itself, for it caused the population to pour in thousands from the narrow lanes with which this human warren is intersected. There seemed a danger that we might be stopped by the mere pressure of the crowd, so I gave the word to whip up our steeds, and we dashed along, regardless of whom we knocked over.

Just as we reached the gate on the Chemulpo road the great bell began to ring, the bell which every night at sunset orders the closing of the gates. The big doors were being slowly closed as we approached, and here my two Japanese again gave striking proof of their value. They dashed forward, and, in spite of the ringing of the bell, ordered the guards to fling wide the portal, but upon the guards showing some hesitation, the foremost Japanese at once shot one of them in his tracks, whereupon the rest fled. We squeezed through, and the Japanese proposed we should close the gates completely, so that the crowd might be kept in, but this proved impossible, because they could be fastened only on the inside, and we had no means of assuring ourselves that the gates would remain shut. There was therefore nothing for it but a race for Chemulpo, twenty-six miles away. Before we had gone a dozen yards the pressure of the crowd opened the gates wide, and the howling mob poured through like a resistless torrent.

I now re-arranged my party, asking Mr. Hemster to take the lead, while the two Japanese and myself fought a retreating battle with the multitude that followed us. The Corean man is a stalwart individual with sturdy legs that are almost untiring in a race. While cowards individually, they become dangerous in the mass, and I continually urged our people to gallop as hard as they could, with the double purpose of exhausting all but the most strenuous in our pursuit, and of preventing the outskirts of the mob on either hand from out-flanking us. For the first three miles or so our re-volver-shots kept them at a respectful distance, but after five or six miles had been accomplished, and the crowd showed no signs of fatigue, while our ammuni-tion began to run low, I realized that I must do some-thing to save the rest from capture.

Leaving the two Japanese as an efficient rearguard, I galloped forward to Mr. Hemster, and gave him de-tails of my plan, which I had some difficulty in getting him to accept. In fact he did accept it only on my assurance that there was no real danger to myself. Bidding a hasty farewell to the ladies, I dropped again to the rear. Each of the Japanese had tethered to his horse's bridle a rope attached to a pony carrying our strings of cash. I untied these ponies, and attached them to my own mount, ordering the Japanese to take the van once more; and, as they were residents of Chemulpo, and therefore knew the road perfectly, I told them to lead the party as quickly as they could into safety, promising them a large additional reward for doing so.

The rest now galloped on, leaving me standing in the middle of the road, with three horses under my charge. The bellowing mob seemed nonplussed by this movement, and, apparently fearing a trap of some kind, came to a halt. There was not bravery enough among them even to attack one man at close quarters, although they might have overwhelmed him by simply moving in bulk upon him. Each of the two led-horses carried something like twenty thousand sek, strung in ropes of five hundred each, so knotted that the cash is divided into sections of a hundred each. I took my pocket-knife and cut off the first knot, and, grasping the two ends of the string, flung it lasso-wise around my head, and then let go the cut end, causing the hundred cash to shoot into the air like the bursting of a sky-rocket. These people, after all, were merely like children with two dominant qualities, a love of cruelty, and an unlimited avarice,— possibly avarice has the greatest hold upon their affections, and this belief was the basis of my adventure.

Now ensued the strangest battle that ever was fought by mankind, a struggle which Mr. Hemster himself should have appreciated because he had engaged in it time and again in his own country, a battle in which one man with money stood against the bulk of the people. When the shower of a hundred cash was flung above the heads of the mob there ensued one of the wildest struggles it has ever been my fate to witness. I cut the second knot, and flung the second lot of cash far to the left, to check the advance of the crowd that way, which it very effectually did. Then the third knot was severed, and the third lot of coins went spinning through the air to the right. Even before the first string was gone, my party had long since disappeared toward the west. Of course this congregation of heathens could have availed themselves at once of my whole available stock by merely pressing forward, but this thought either never occurred to them, or they were too cowardly to put it into practice. As soon as the flung cash was secured and the scattered stock picked up, two and two fighting for the possession of one miserable coin, a shout arose from them which was the cry of Oliver Twist for "more." And so I played David against that Goliath of a crowd until I began to fear that my arm which whirled the sling would become helpless through exhaustion.

My idea had been, of course, to put the whip to my horse and make for the port after my party, but very soon this project proved to be impossible. I was standing on a slight elevation in the road, and, in spite of my throwing the coins right and left, the two wings of this

tatterdemalion army gradually enfolded me, and before
my fortune was more than half scattered I found myself completely outflanked and surrounded. But no
one made a dash; there was left a respectable circular
clear space about me, the circumference of which was
never nearer than twenty or thirty feet from where I
stood. Moreover I was thankful to see that even those
to the west, who had a free way toward Chemulpo, did
not attempt to break toward the coast. They were all too
eager to get a share of the spoil to mind what became
of the rest of the party, and by the time we had been
an hour or more at this flinging of largesse every individual of them knew that pursuit was hopeless, and by
the same token I knew also that the least danger threat-
ening me was being carried back to Seoul. The crowd
had become riotously good natured, but I knew their
changeableness too well to consider myself safe on that
account. They were as like as not to take me back to
Seoul in a hundred pieces. I began to think seriously
of the future when I came to the last string of cash
on the pony beside me. There was still twenty thousand
on the other nag; but, when that was gone, this mob,
which had no sense of gratitude, were as like to cut my
throat as not. So when I came to the last hundred
sek on the first pony, scattered like grape-shot through
the air, I took advantage of the struggle that ensued to
remount my own nag. There was at once a howl of
rage at this, especially from those to the west of me,
who expected me to attempt escape in that direction.
They stiffened up, and shook fists and sticks at this
supposed intention on my part to cheat them of their

just dues. Never since the Corean kingdom was founded had there been such a distribution of wealth as was now taking place. Heretofore the office-holders had accumulated everything in sight, and naturally the populace was indignant that this enchanting scattering of money should cease while there was still a horse-load of it within reach. I raised my right hand for silence, and then raised my voice and addressed them:

"Gentlemen," said I, "the next hurling of coin takes place at the gates of Seoul. If you are good enough to march quietly with me, I shall relieve the tedium of the way by an occasional contribution. So, my braves, let us get back to the capital."

Capital was what they were after, and so with a howl, which was their nearest approach to a cheer, we set off for Seoul. Tired as my arm was, I occasionally distributed five hundred cash before and behind me, also to the right and left, keeping steadily on, however, until the city was in sight. Then to my dismay, I saw that the great gate was closed. The mob ahead of me had noticed the barred gate before I did, and set up a wail like a lot of lost children. Instantly the cash distribution was forgotten, and panic seized them. They were locked out, and no one knew what might be happening inside. The tolling of the big bell still boomed through the air, but only occasionally, bearing some resemblance to a funeral knell. Because the gate was shut these people had not reasoning powers enough to surmise that the other gates were shut also, and in a magic way the huge mob began to dissolve and disappear, scampering over rocks and stones to find out whether the whole city was hermetically sealed or not. There was a group of people on the wall above the gate, and someone had shouted that the northern port was open. This statement was undoubtedly false, but the official who cried it evidently thought it was safer to dismiss the mob as he could. In a few minutes I found myself practically alone, and then was amazed beyond measure to hear a voice from above the gate call down to me :

" For Heaven's sake, Tremorne, is that you? "

CHAPTER XV

I LOOKED up, and saw leaning toward me Wallace Carmichel, the British Consul-General in Seoul, an efficient man whom I had not met for five years, when he was in the Embassy at Pekin. At once there flashed through my mind Mr. Hemster's desire that I should not mention our plight to the Consuls of either his country or my own, so I resolved on the instant to keep to myself, if possible, the mission that had brought me to the capital. Indeed within the last few minutes the whole situation had changed. I had no desire to return to Seoul, and only retreated because I was compelled to do so; but now the way was perfectly clear between me and Chemulpo on turning my horse around. Yet Carmichel would think it exceedingly strange if I could not give some excuse for marching up to the gate of Seoul and marching down again, like the historical general on the hill. I wished he had remained at his Consulate, yet there he was, beaming down upon me, so I took momentary refuge in airy persiflage.

"Hullo, Carmichel, how goes it? Has the early-closing movement been adopted in Seoul? It is n't Saturday afternoon, is it?"

"No, it is n't," he replied, "and if you 'll take the advice of an old friend, you 'll turn your horse's head, and make straight back for Chemulpo. I think we 're in for a rather nasty time here, if you ask me."

" I do ask you. What 's wrong ? "

I was anxious to learn whether he knew anything of the escape of our party in the early morning; but even if he had been told about it, the Coreans are such un-mitigated liars that it is not likely he would have be-lieved them if he had not himself seen the procession, and I very much doubted if he had done so, for Car-michel was never afflicted with the early-rising habit. I was, however, wholly unprepared for his amazing reply.

" The Empress of Corea was assassinated last night," he said. " I imagine they don't want the news to spread. The Palace is closed, and all the gates of the city were shut before I was up this morning. The Court *entourage* is trying to pretend that the Empress died a natural death, but I have it on as good authority as anything can be had in this mendacious place that the Empress was literally cut to pieces."

" Good God ! " I cried. " Can that be true ? "

" Anything may be true in this forsaken hole. I heard you had left the service. Came into a fortune, eh? Lucky devil! I wish I were in your shoes! This is worse than China, and that was bad enough. I suppose you are here on private business. Well, take a friend's advice and get back. Nothing can be done here for a while, any how."

" I 'll take your advice, Carmichel. Is there any message I can carry for you to Chemulpo ? "

" No, you may tell them what 's happened."

"Are you in any danger, do you think?"

"I don't think so. Of course, one can never tell what may turn up in this beastly place. I've got the Consulate well guarded, and we can stand a siege. I heard that there was a mob approaching the town, and so came up to see what it was all about. Where are you stopping at Chemulpo?"

"I have been yachting with a friend of mine, and his craft is in the harbour there."

"Well, if you've no business in Seoul, I advise you to get back to the yacht. You'll be safer on the sea than in Corea."

"I believe you!"

"How did you come to be in the midst of that Bank Holiday gang, Tremorne?" asked the Consul, his curiosity evidently rising.

"Oh, they overtook me, so we came along together."

"It's a wonder they didn't rob you of all you possess."

"I forestalled that by scattering something like twenty thousand sek among them. I thought I'd be all right when I came to the gate, but was rather taken aback to find it closed."

"Twenty thousand sek! And I suppose you don't mind throwing it away any more than a handful of ha' pence! Lucky beggar! And yachting around the world with a millionaire friend, I expect. Well, life's easy for some people," said the Consul-General with a sigh.

I laughed at him, and wondered what he would have said had he known the truth.

"Sure you don't want me to send a guard up from Chemulpo for you?"

"No, I don't think our consulate will be the storm-center here. I rather imagine the tornado will rage around the residence of our Japanese friends. The Coreans say that a Japanese killed one of the guards here this morning at the gate, but the Japanese Minister insists that all of his countrymen in the city are accounted for, and that this allegation of murder is a lie, which I have not the least doubt it is. I heard a lot of promiscuous firing this morning before I was up, but it seemed to me all in the direction of the Palace. They are eternally raising some shindy here, and blaming it on decent people. I'm sorry to see you turn back, Tremorne, but a man who isn't compelled to stay here is wise to avoid such diggings. If you return you'll call on me, won't you?"

"Oh, certainly," said I, gathering up the reins. "So long, Carmichel, and be as good to yourself as you can."

Saying this I turned toward Chemulpo, and reached it very late that night. The journey was one of the most disagreeable I had ever taken, for my right arm —I suppose through the straining of the muscles— became utterly helpless and very painful. It swelled so, especially at the shoulder, that I feared I should have to cut the sleeve of my coat. David was more fortunate than I, because he did his business with one shot: my giant required continual shooting, and now I was suffering for it. If I had been attacked, I should have found myself completely helpless; but fortunately the way was clear, and with my three steeds I came through without mishap. Before going on board I searched out my two Japanese, and found, as I expected, that Mr. Hemster had rewarded them with a liberality that took their breath away. He had paid them for the three horses, which he looked upon as lost, and now I turned the nags over to them, together with the twenty thousand sek that was on one of them; so the brave, resourceful little men had no complaint to make regarding lack of recognition.

I had not intended to go aboard the yacht that night, but Mr. Hemster had made the Japs promise to show a flare if any news came of me, and in the morning he was going to organize an expedition for my rescue. As soon as I encountered my Japs one of them ran for a torch and set it afire. It was at once answered by a rocket from the yacht, and before I had finished my conversation with him I heard the measured beat of the oars in the water, and found that in spite of his fatigue the kindly old man himself had come ashore for me. He tried to shake hands, but I warded him off with my left arm, laughing as I did so, and told him my right would not be in condition for some time yet. As we rowed out to the yacht I told him all that had happened, and informed him about the murder of the Empress, which news my Japanese friends were commissioned to proclaim in Chemulpo, as I had promised the British Consul. Mr. Hemster was much affected by this news, and I saw plainly that he considered his ill-fated expedition to have been the probable cause of this unfortunate lady's taking off.

I was nearly famished when we reached the steamer, for I had had nothing since early morning but a ham sandwich I had put in my pocket. The bag of provisions intended for consumption on the way had been carried by the Chinese cook, and at the moment of parting I had thought nothing of the commissariat, which was extremely poor generalship on my part, and an omission which caused me sorrow later in the day.

Sitting in the boat after my exertions left me so stiff and unwieldy that one of the sailors had to help me up the side, and, stepping on deck, I staggered, and would have fallen if he had not caught me. The waning moon had risen, but the light was not strong. I saw a shadowy figure make for the companion-way, then stop with a little cry, and run forward to where I stood.

"You are wounded, Mr. Tremorne!" she cried.

"No, Miss Stretton, I am all right, except my arm, and its disablement is rather a joke than otherwise."

"He is wounded, is he not, Mr. Hemster?" appealed the girl, as the old man came up the gangway.

"Tut, tut, child! You should have been in bed long ago! He isn't wounded, but he's nearly starved to death through our taking away all the provisions with us when we deserted him."

"Oh, dear!" she cried. "Then you didn't find the bag."

"What bag?" I asked.

"When we were having lunch Mr. Hemster remembered that you were unprovided for, so we raised a cairn of stones by the wayside and left a bag of provisions on top of it, hoping you would recognize it, for Mr. Hemster felt sure you would win through somehow or other. You would be extremely flattered, Mr. Tremorne, if you knew what faith he has in you."

I laughed and told her I was glad to hear it.

" Tut, tut! " said the old man. " Don't stand idly chattering here when there 's a first-rate supper spread out for you down below. Away you go. I must have a word with the captain, for we are off to Nagasaki within ten minutes, so I shall bid you both good-night."

I took it very kindly of the old gentleman to leave us thus alone, and I have no doubt he thought of his own younger days when he did so. I wickedly pretended a greater weakness than I actually felt, and so Miss Stretton kindly supported me with her arm, and thus we went down the stairway together, where, as the old gentleman had said, I found one of the most delicious cold collations I had ever encountered, flanked by a bottle of his very finest champagne. I persuaded Miss Stretton to sit down opposite me, which, after some demur about the lateness of the hour, she consented to do, for I told her my right arm was absolutely helpless, and the left almost equally awkward.

" So," I said, " you must prove yourself a ministering angel now."

" Ah, that," she said, " is when pain and anguish wring the brow. As I understand it, pain and anguish wring the arm. Please tell me how it happened."

Under the deft manipulation of the Japanese boy,

the champagne ccrk came out with a pop, and, as if it
were a signal-gun, there immediately followed the rattle of the anchor-chain coming up, and almost before
my story was begun, we heard the steady throb-throb
of the engine, and it sent a vibration of thankfulness
through my aching frame.

"You do look haggard and worn," she said; "and
I think I must insist on regarding you rather in the
light of a hero."

"Oh, there was nothing heroic in flinging cheap
cash about in the reckless way I did. I was never in
any real danger."

"I think we have all been in danger, more or less,
since we entered those Palace gates. Although I said
nothing I could see from your face what you were
thinking."

"Yes, I know of old your uncanny proclivities in
mind-reading. Now that every pulsation of the engine
is carrying us farther away from that plague-spot of
earth, there is no harm in saying that I spent some
days and nights of deep anxiety, and that, I assure you,
not on my own account."

"I quite believe you," said the young lady, raising
her eyes for a moment, and gazing down on the tablecloth again. Then she looked brightly up once more,
and said archly:

"I hope it won't make you conceited, but I walked
the deck to-night with fear tugging at my heart. I
don't think I ever was so glad in my life as when
I saw the flare, as had been arranged, and knew you
were safe. When I heard you talking to Mr. Hemster

in the boat, your voice floated over the water very distinctly, and I think I breathed a little expression of gratitude."

"Hilda," said I, leaning across the table, "it is very kind of you to say that."

Here, to my annoyance, the Japanese boy came into the saloon, although I had told him I had no further need for him that night. He approached us, and said respectfully, and I am sure somewhat unwillingly:

"Miss Hemster's compliments, sir, and she wishes you would stop chattering here all night long, so that people could get to sleep."

Miss Stretton sprang to her feet, a crimson flush coming into her face.

"Thank Miss Hemster for me," said I to the Japanese, "and inform her that we will finish our conversation on deck."

"No, no!" cried Hilda peremptorily; "it is terribly late, and it is too bad of me keeping you talking here when you should be resting. I assure you I did not intend to remain on deck after I had learned of your safe arrival."

"I know that, Hilda. It was when you saw me stagger that, like the kind-hearted girl you are, you came forward. Now, do come up on deck with me, if only for five minutes."

"No, no," she repeated in a whisper.

Forgetting the condition of my arm, I made an effort to encircle her. She whisked herself silently away, but, hearing the groan that involuntarily escaped me when the helpless arm struck the table and sent an electric spasm of pain to my shoulder, she turned rapidly toward me with pity in her face. Then, springing forward, she raised her lips to mine for one infinitesimal fraction of a second, and almost before the rest of that moment of bliss was passed I found myself alone in the empty saloon.

CHAPTER XVI

LATE as it was, I went up on deck, and it was lucky for me I did so, for I met our bluff old captain, who, when he learned of the disablement of my arm, said genially that he had a Cape Cod liniment good for man or donkey, and I was welcome to it in either capacity. He ordered me down to my stateroom, and followed later with the bottle. His own gnarled hands rubbed the pungent-smelling stuff on my arm, and he told me I'd be next to all right in the morning, which prophecy came true.

I am sorry that in these voyages to and from Corea we met absolutely no adventures, picked up no shipwrecked crew, and met no cyclone, so I am unable to write down any of those vivid descriptions that I have always admired in Mr. Clark Russell.

Next morning was heavenly in its beauty and its calm. Nagasaki was the last civilized address which would receive telegrams, letters or papers for Mr. Hemster, and the old gentleman was anxious to reach there as soon as possible. As I have remarked before, he was constantly yearning for a daily paper. The captain informed me that he had engaged a " heathen Chinee " as pilot, and so was striking direct from Chemulpo to Nagasaki, letting the islands take care of themselves, as he remarked.

A CHICAGO PRINCESS

I walked the deck, watching eagerly for the coming of Hilda Stretton, but instead there arrived Gertrude Hemster, bright, smiling, and beautiful. I was just now regretting lack of opportunity to indulge in Clark-Russellism, yet here was a chance for a descriptive writer which proved quite beyond my powers. The costume of Miss Hemster was bewildering in its Parisian completeness. That girl must have had a storehouse of expensive gowns aboard the yacht. I suppose this was what a writer in a lady's paper would call a confection, or a creation, or something of that sort; but so far as I am concerned you might as well expect an elucidation of higher mathematics as an adequate delineation of that sumptuous gown. All I can say is that the *tout ensemble* was perfect, and the girl herself was radiant in her loveliness. She approached me with a winning smile like that of an angel.

" I want you to know how I appreciate your bravery. I shall never forget,—no, not if I live to be a thousand years old,—how grand and noble you looked standing up alone against that horde of savages. I was just telling Poppa that the very first reporter he meets, he must give a glowing account to him of your heroism."

I have always noted that when Miss Hemster was in extreme good humour she referred to the old gentleman as Poppa; on other occasions she called him Father. The project of giving away my adventures to the newspapers did not in the least commend itself to me.

" Good-morning, Miss Hemster," I said, " I am extremely pleased to see you looking so well after a somewhat arduous day."

"It was rather a trying time, wasn't it?" she replied sweetly, "and if I look well it's because of the dress, I think. How do you like it?" and she stepped back with a sweeping curtesy that would have done credit to an actress, and took up an attitude that displayed her drapery to the very best advantage.

"It is heavenly," I said; "never in my life have I seen anything to compare with it,—or with the wearer," I added.

"How sweet of you to say that!" she murmured, looking up at me archly, with a winning, bird-like movement. A glorified bird-of-paradise she seemed, and there was no denying it. With a touching pathetic note in her voice she continued,—very humbly, if one might judge,— "You haven't been a bit nice to me lately. I have wondered why you were so unkind."

"Believe me, Miss Hemster," I said, "I have not intended to be unkind, and I am very sorry if I have appeared so. You must remember we have been thrown into very trying circumstances, and as I was probably better acquainted with the conditions than any one of our party I always endeavoured to give the best advice I could, which sometimes, alas, ran counter to your own wishes. It seemed to me now and then you did not quite appreciate the danger which threatened us, and you also appeared to have a distrust of me, which, I may tell you, was entirely unfounded."

"Of course it was," she cried contritely, "but nevertheless I always had the utmost confidence in you, although you see I'm so impulsive that I always say the first thing that comes into my head, and that gives people a wrong idea about me. You take everything so seriously and make no allowances. I think at heart you 're a very hard man."

" Oh, I hope not."

" Yes, you are. You have numerous little rules, and you measure everybody by them. I seem to feel that you are mentally sizing me up, and that makes me say horrid things."

" If that is the case, I must try to improve my character."

" Oh, I 'm not blaming you at all, only telling you the way it strikes me. Perhaps I 'm altogether wrong. Very likely I am and anyhow I don't suppose it does any good to talk of these things. By the way, how is your arm this morning? "

" It is all right, thank you. The captain's liniment has been magical in its effect. It was very stupid of me to get my arm in such a condition, and there is less excuse because I used to be a first-rate cricket bowler; but somehow yesterday I got so interested in the game that I forgot about my muscles."

" Is it true that the Empress has been murdered? "

" Yes, I had the news from the British Consul, and I have no doubt of its accuracy."

" How perfectly awful to think that only the day before yesterday we saw her sitting there like a graven image; indeed she scarcely seemed alive even then. What in the world did they kill the poor woman for? "

" I do not know," I replied, although I had strong suspicions regarding the cause of her fate. The next statement by Miss Hemster astonished me.

"Well, it served her right. A woman in that position should assert herself. She sat there like a Chinese doll that had gone to sleep. If she had made them stand around they would have had more respect for her. Any woman owes it to her sex to make the world respect her. Think of a sleepy creature like that holding the position of Empress, and yet making less than nothing of it."

"You must remember, Miss Hemster, that the status of woman in Corea is vastly different from her position in the United States."

"Well, and whose fault is that? It is the fault of the women. We demand our rights in the States, and get them. If this creature at Seoul had been of any use in the world she would have revolutionized the status of women,—at least within the bounds of her own kingdom."

I ventured to remark that Oriental ideas of women were of a low order, and that, as the women themselves were educated to accept this state of things, nothing much should be expected of them.

"Oh, nonsense!" cried Miss Hemster strenuously; "look at the Empress of China. She makes people stand around. Then there was Catherine of Russia, and goodness knows Russia's far enough behind in its ideas! But Catherine did n't mind that; she just walked in, and made herself feared by the whole world. A few more women like that in the Orient would bring these heathen people to their senses. It serves this Corean Queen right when you think of the opportunity she had, and the way she misused it, sitting there like a great lump of dough strung around with jewels she could not appreciate, like a wax figure in a ten-cent show. I have no patience with such animals."

I thought this judgment of Miss Hemster's rather harsh, but experience had taught me not to be rash in expressing my opinion; so we conversed amicably about many things until the gong rang for luncheon. I must say that hers was a most attractive personality when she exerted herself to please. At luncheon she was the life of the party, making the captain laugh outrageously, and even bringing a smile now and then to her father's grave face, although it seemed to me he watched her furtively under his shaggy eyebrows now and then as if apprehensive that this mood might not last,—somewhat fearful, I imagine, regarding what might follow. I could not help noticing that there was a subtle change in the old gentleman's attitude toward his daughter, and I fancied that her exuberant spirits were perhaps forced to the front, to counteract in a measure this new attitude. I thought I detected now and then a false note in her hilarity, but perhaps that may have been a delusion of my imagination, such as it is. After the captain had gone, toward the end of the meal, her father seemed to be endeavouring silently to attract her attention; but she rattled on in almost breathless haste, talking flippantly to Miss Stretton and myself alternately, and never once looking toward the head of the table. I surmised that there was something beneath all this with which I was not acquainted, and that there was going on before me a silent contest of two wills, the latent determination of the father op-

posed to the unconcealed stubbornness of the daughter.
I sympathized with the old man, because I was myself
engaged in a mental endeavour to cause Hilda Stretton
to look across at me, but hitherto without success. Not
a single glance had I received during the meal. At
last the old gentleman rose, and stood hesitating, as if
he wished to make a plunge; then, finally, he interrupted the rattle of conversation by saying:

"Gertrude, I wish to have a few words with you in
my office."

"All right, Poppa, I'll be there in a minute," she replied nonchalantly.

"I want you to come *now*," he said, with more
sternness in his voice than I had ever heard there before. For one brief moment I feared we were going
to have a scene, but Miss Gertrude merely laughed joyously and sprang to her feet, saying, "I'll race you to
the office then," and disappeared down the passage aft
almost before her sentence was ended. Mr. Hemster
slowly followed her.

Hilda Stretton half rose, as if to leave me there
alone, then sat down again, and courageously looked
me full in the face across the table.

"He is too late," she whispered.

"Too late for what?" I asked.

"Too late in exerting parental authority."

"Is he trying to do that?"

"Didn't you see it?"

"Well, if that was his endeavour, he succeeded."

"For the moment, yes. He thinks he's going to
talk to her, but it is she who will talk to him, and she

186

preferred doing it this time in the privacy of the room he calls his office. A moment more, and he would have learned her opinion of him before witnesses. I am very glad it did not come to that, but the trouble is merely postponed. Poor old gentleman, I wish I could help him! He does not understand his daughter in the least. But let us go on deck and have coffee there."

" I was just going to propose that," I cried, delighted, springing to my feet. We went up the stair together and I placed a little wicker table well forward, with a wicker chair on each side of it, taking a position on deck as far from the companion-way as possible, so that we should not be surprised by any one coming up from below. The Japanese boy served our coffee, and when he was gone Hilda continued her subject, speaking very seriously.

" He does not understand her at all, as I have said. Since she was a baby she has had her own way in everything, without check or hindrance from him, and of course no one else dared to check or hinder her. Now she is more than twenty-one years of age, and if he imagines that discipline can be enforced at this late hour he is very much mistaken."

" Is he trying to enforce discipline? "

" Yes, he is. He has foolishly made up his mind that it will be for the girl's good. That, of course, is all he thinks of,—dear, generous-hearted man that he is! But if he goes on there will be a tragedy, and I want you to warn him."

" I dare not interfere, Hilda."

187

"Why not? Haven't you a very great liking for him?"

"Yes, I have. I would do almost anything in the world for him."

"Then do what I tell you."

"What is it?"

"See him privately in his office, and tell him to leave his daughter alone. Warn him that if he does not there will be a tragedy."

"Tell me exactly what you mean."

"She will commit suicide."

This statement, solemnly given, seemed to me so utterly absurd that it relieved the tension which was creeping into the occasion. I leaned back in my chair and laughed until I saw a look of pained surprise come into Hilda's face, which instantly sobered me.

"Really, Hilda, you are the very best girl in the world, yet it is you who do not understand that young woman. She is too thoroughly selfish to commit suicide, or to do anything else to her own injury."

"Suicide," said Hilda gravely, "is not always a matter of calculation, but often the act of a moment of frenzy,—at least so it will be in Gertrude Hemster's case if her father now attempts to draw tight the reins of authority. He will madden her, and you have no conception of the depth of bitterness that is in her nature. If it occurs to her in her next extravagant tantrum that by killing herself she will break her father's heart, which undoubtedly would be the case, she is quite capable of plunging into the sea, or sending a revolver bullet through her head. I have been convinced of this for some time past, but I never thought her father would be so ill-advised as to change the drifting line of conduct he has always held in regard to her."

"My dear Hilda, you are not consistent. Do you remember an occasion, which to tell the truth I am loth to recall, when you said if her father treated her as I had done her character would be much more amiable than it now appears to be?"

"I don't think I said that, Mr. Tremorne. I may have hinted that if her father had taken a more strenuous attitude in the past, he would not have such a difficult task before him in the present, or I may have said that a husband might tame the shrew. The latter, I believe, would lead to either a reformation or the divorce court, I don't quite know which. Or perhaps even then there might be a tragedy; but it would be the husband who would suffer, not herself. A man she married might control her. It would really be an interesting experiment, and no one can predict whether it would turn out well or ill; but her father cannot control her because all these years of affectionate neglect are behind him, years in which he was absorbed in business, leaving the forming of her character to hirelings, thinking that because he paid them well they would do their duty, whereas the high salary merely made them anxious to retain their positions at any cost of flattery and indulgence to their pupil."

"Then, Hilda, why don't you speak to him about it? You have known him for more years than I have days, and I am sure he would take it kindlier from you than from me."

"To tell you the truth, I have spoken to him. I spoke to him last night when we were both waiting for that flare from the shore at Chemulpo. I could not tell whether my talk had any effect or not, for he said nothing, beyond thanking me for my advice. I see to-day that it has had no effect. So now I beg you to try."

"But if you failed, how could I hope to succeed?"

"I 'll tell you why. In the first place because you are the cause of this change of attitude on the part of Mr. Hemster."

"I the cause?"

"Certainly. He has undoubtedly a great liking for you, in spite of the fact that he has known you so short a time. In some unexplainable way he has come to look at his daughter through your eyes, and I think he is startled at the vision he has seen. But he does not take sufficient account of the fact that he is not dealing now with a little girl, but with a grown woman. I noticed the gradual change in his manner during our stay at the Palace, and it became much more marked on the way back to Chemulpo, after we had left you alone battling with the savages of Seoul. You have said you were in no real danger, but Mr. Hemster did not think so, and he seemed greatly impressed by the fact that a comparative stranger should cheerfully insist on jeopardizing his life for the safety of our party, and to my deep anxiety his demeanour toward his daughter was at first severe and then harsh, for he roundly accused her of being the cause of our difficulties. I shall pass over the storm that ensued, merely saying that it took our whole force to prevent Miss Hemster from returning to Seoul."

"Great Heavens!" I exclaimed, "surely that was mere pretence on her part; sheer bravado."

"Not altogether. It was grim determination to do the thing that would immediately hurt her father, and I do not know what would have happened if she had escaped from us. It had the instant effect of subduing him, bringing him practically to his knees before her. So she sulked all the way to Chemulpo, and I expected that the brief assumption of authority had ended; but while we were rowing out to the yacht he spoke very sharply to her, and I saw with regret that his determination was at least equal to hers. Therefore I spoke to him after she had gone to her room, and he said very little one way or the other. Now he appears to think that as he has got her safely on his yacht once more he can bend her to his will, and I am terrified at the outlook."

"Well, it does n't look enticing, does it?"

"No, it does n't, so won't you please talk with him for his own sake?"

"I'd rather face the Emperor of Corea again, or his amiable subjects in mass meeting assembled, but I 'll do it for your sake. Oh, yes, and for his sake, too; I would do anything I could to make matters easy for Mr. Hemster."

"Thank you so much," said the girl simply, leaning back in her chair with a sigh of contentment. "Now let us talk of something else."

"With all my heart, Hilda. I 've been wanting to

talk of something else ever since your very abrupt departure last night. Now am I over-confident in taking your last brief action there as equivalent to the monosyllable 'Yes'?"

The girl laughed and coloured, visibly embarrassed. She darted a quick glance at me, then veiled her eyes again.

"The brief action, as you call it, seems rather impulsive now in the glare of daylight, and was equivalent to much more than the monosyllable 'Yes.' Three times as much. It was equivalent to the trisyllable 'Sympathy.' I was merely expressing sympathy."

"Was that all?"

"Wasn't that more than enough? I have thought since, with shame, that my action was just a trifle overbold, and I fear you are of the same opinion, although too kind-hearted to show it."

"My whole thought was a protest against its brevity."

"But brevity is the soul of wit, you know."

"Yes, Hilda," said I, leaning forward toward her, "but not the soul of kissing. If my right arm had not temporarily lost its power you had never escaped with the celerity you did. 'Man wants but little here below,' and I want that little monosyllable rather than the large trisyllable. Make me for ever happy by saying you meant it."

"For ever is a long time," she answered dreamily, her eyes partially closed.

"*Miss Stretton, will you oblige me by going downstairs; I wish to talk to Mr. Tremorne.*"

" Yes, Hilda," said I, " but not the soul of kissing."

A CHICAGO PRINCESS

The words, sharp and decisive, cut like a knife, and, starting to my feet in amazement, I saw that Gertrude Hemster stood before us, her brow a thundercloud. Turning from her beautiful but forbidding countenance to see the effect of her peremptory sentence upon my dear companion, I found the chair empty, and the space around me vacant as if she had vanished into invisibility through the malign incantation of a sorceress.

CHAPTER XVII

"WILL you be seated, Miss Hemster?" I said with such calmness as I could bring to my command.

"No, I won't," she snapped, like the click of a rifle.

I don't know why it is that this girl always called forth hitherto unsuspected discourtesy which I regret to admit seems to lie very deep in my nature. I was bitterly angry at her rude dismissal of Hilda Stretton.

"Oh, very well; stand then!" I retorted with inexcusable lack of chivalry, and, that my culpability should be complete, immediately slammed myself emphatically down into the chair from which I had just risen. As I came down with a thump that made the wicker chair groan in protest, the look the lady bestowed upon me must have resembled that of the Medusa which turned people into stone.

"Well, you *are* polite, I must say," she exclaimed, with a malicious swish of her skirts as she walked to and fro before me.

"You so monopolize all politeness on board this yacht," was my unmannerly rejoinder, "that there is none of it left for the rest of us."

She stopped in her rapid walk and faced me.

"You 're a brute," she said deliberately.

"You expressed that opinion before. Why not try something original?"

"Do you think that is a gentlemanly remark to make?" she asked.

"No, I don't. Some years of vagabondage coupled with more recent events have destroyed all claim I ever possessed to being a gentleman."

"You admit, then, you are the scum of the earth."

"Oh, certainly."

Suddenly she flounced herself down in the chair Hilda had occupied, and stared at me for a few moments. Then she said in a voice much modified:

"What were you and Miss Stretton discussing so earnestly when I came up?"

"Did n't you hear?"

"No. I am no eavesdropper, but I know you were talking of me."

"Ah, then you did n't hear."

"I told you I did n't, but I tell you what I suspect."

"Then your suspicions are entirely unfounded, Miss Hemster."

"I don't believe it, but I 'll say this for you; however much of a beast you may be, you are rather unhandy at a lie; so if you wish to convince me that you are speaking the truth, you must tell me, without taking time to consider, what you were talking about if you were not talking of me."

All this was uttered at lightning speed.

"I need no time for consideration to answer that question. We were talking of ourselves."

"What were you saying? Come now, out with it if you dare. I can see by your face you are trying to make up something."

"Really, you underestimate my courage, Miss Hemster. I was asking Hilda Stretton to do me the honour of marrying me, and she was about to reply when you cut short a conference so absorbing that we had not noticed your approach."

This explanation seemed to be so unexpected that for a moment the young woman sat breathless and expressionless. Then she gradually sank back in her chair with closed eyes, all colour leaving her face.

Now, I am well aware of the effect the words just written will have on the mind of the indulgent reader. She will think I 'm trying to hint that the girl, despite her actions, was in love with me. I beg to state that I am no such conceited ass as the above paragraph would imply. My wife has always held that Gertrude Hemster *was* in love with me, but that is merely the prejudiced view of an affectionate woman, and I have ever strenuously combated it. The character of Gertrude Hemster has for long been a puzzle to me, and I can hardly expect the credence of the reader when I say that I have toned down her words and actions rather than exaggerated them. But my own theory of the case is this: Miss Hemster had an inordinate love of conquest and power. I think I should have got along better with her if I had proposed to her and taken my rejection in a broken and contrite spirit. That she would have rejected me, I am as positive as that I breathe. I am equally certain that, while she would have scorned to acknowledge me as a favoured lover, she was nevertheless humiliated to know that I had given preference to one upon whom she rather looked down,—one whom she regarded as a recipient of her own bounty,—and the moment I made my confession I was sorry I had done so, for Hilda's sake.

It has also been hinted,—I shall not say by whom,—that I was on a fair way of being in love with Gertrude Hemster if everything had progressed favourably. I need hardly point out to the reader the utter erroneousness of this surmise. I do not deny that during the first day of our acquaintance I was greatly attracted by her, or perhaps I should say wonderfully interested in her. I had never met any one just like her before, nor have I since for that matter. But that I was even on the verge of being in love with her I emphatically deny. I have no hesitation in confessing that she was the most beautiful woman I have ever seen, when it pleased her to be gracious. She would certainly have made a superb actress if Fortune had cast her rôle upon the stage. But, as I have said, I never understood this woman, or comprehended her lightning changes of character. I do not know to this day whether she was merely a shallow vixen or a creature of deep though uncontrolled passion. I therefore content myself with setting down here, as accurately as possible, what happened on the various occasions of which I speak, so that each reader may draw her own conclusions, if indeed there are any conclusions to be drawn, and I do this as truthfully as may be, at the risk of some misunderstanding of my own position, as in the present instance.

The silence which followed my announcement was at last broken by a light sarcastic laugh.

197

"Really, Mr. Tremorne," she said, "it is not very flattering to me to suppose that I am interested in the love affairs of the servants' hall."

I bowed my acknowledgment of this thrust.

"My statement, Miss Hemster, was not made for your entertainment, or with any hope that it would engage your attention, but merely as an answer to your direct question."

"So two penniless paupers are going to unite their fortunes!"

"Penniless, only relatively so; paupers, no."

"Nothing added to nothing makes how much, Mr. Tremorne?"

"Madam, I am an Oxford man."

"What has that to do with it?"

"Much. Cambridge is the mathematical university. I never was good at figures."

"Perhaps that 's why you threw away your money."

"Perhaps. Still, the money I threw away yesterday belonged to your father."

"Is that to remind me of the debt I am supposed to owe you?"

"You owe me nothing. If anybody owes me anything I am certain Mr. Hemster will discharge the debt with his usual generosity."

"Oh, you are counting on that, are you?"

"We have Biblical assurance, Miss Hemster, of the fact that the labourer is worthy of his hire. My hire is all I expect, and all I shall accept."

"Well, it is my hope that your term of employment will be as short as possible; therefore I ask you to resign your position as soon as we reach Nagasaki. Your presence on this ship is odious to me."

"I am sorry for that."

"Then you won't resign?"

"I say that I am sorry my presence on this ship is odious to you."

"You can at once solve the problem by resigning, as I have suggested."

"I dispute your right to make suggestions to me. If you want me to leave the yacht, ask your father to discharge me."

"There is always a certain humiliation in abrupt dismissal. If you do not go voluntarily, and without telling my father that I have asked you to resign, I shall put Hilda Stretton ashore at Nagasaki with money enough to pay her passage home."

"How generous of you! First-class or steerage?"

Her face became a flame of fire, and she clenched her hands till the nails bit the pink palms.

"You sneaking reptile!" she cried, her voice trembling with anger; "you backbiting, underhand beast! What lies have you dared tell my father about me?"

"You are under some strange misapprehension, Miss Hemster," I replied, with a coolness which earned my mental approbation, fervently hoping at the same time that I might continue to maintain control over my deplorable temper; "you have jumped at a conclusion not borne out by fact. I assure you I have never discussed you with your father, and should not venture to do so."

I remembered the moment I had spoken that I had

just promised another lady to do that very thing. What everybody says must be true when they state that my thoughts are awkward and ungainly, rarely coming up to the starting-point until too late. I fear this tardy recollection brought the colour to my face, for the angry eyes of the girl were upon me, and she evidently misread this untimely flushing. She leaned across the little wicker table and said in a calm, unruffled voice, marked with the bitterness of hate:

" You are a liar."

I rose to my feet with the intention of leaving her, but she sprang up with a nimbleness superior to my own, and before I was aware of what she was about she thrust her two hands against my breast and plumped me unexpectedly down into my chair again. It was a ludicrous and humiliating situation, but I was too angry to laugh about it. Standing over me, she hissed down at me:

" You heard what I said."

" Perfectly, and I am resolved that there shall be no further communication between us."

" Oh, are you? Well, you 'll listen to what I have to say, or I 'll add ' coward ' to ' liar.' Either you or Hilda Stretton has been poisoning my father's mind against me. Which was it? "

" It was I, of course."

" Then you admit you are a liar? "

" ' All men are liars,' said the Psalmist, so why should I be an exception? "

" You are very good at quoting the Bible, are n't you? Why don't you live up to it? "

"I should be the better man if I did."

"Will you resign at Nagasaki, then?"

"I shall do exactly what your father orders me to do."

"That is precisely the answer I should have expected from a mud-wallower who came to us from the gutter."

"You are mistaken. I lived up on a hill."

"Well, I give you warning, that if you don't leave this yacht you will regret it."

"I shall probably regret the tender memories of your conversation, Miss Hemster; but if you think to frighten me I beg to point out that it is really yourself who is in danger, as you might know if experience taught the class of persons it is said to teach. You have called me a brute and a beast and all the rest of it, and have partly persuaded me that you are right. Now the danger to you lies in the fact that you will go just a step too far on one of these occasions, and then I shall pick you up and throw you overboard. Now allow me to say that you have about reached the limit, likewise to inform you that I shall not resign."

I now arose, confronting her, and flung the wicker chair to the other side of the deck. Then, taking off my hat, I left her standing there.

CHAPTER XVIII

I AM tired of my own shortcomings, and I have no
doubt the reader is also, if she has read this far.
I shall therefore make no attempt to excuse my
language toward Gertrude Hemster. The heated conversation in which we indulged had, however, one effect upon my future course. I resolved not to say a
word to her father against his treatment of her.
Whatever the old gentleman had said to her, it could
not have been cruder or ruder than the language which
I had myself employed. Therefore I felt it would be
ludicrous for me to act the part of censor or adviser.
I had shown my own unfitness for either of those rôles.
Besides this, I had been convinced that Hilda Stretton
was entirely mistaken in thinking that the young
woman would commit suicide or do any injury to herself. My summing up of her character led me to the
belief that although she would be quite willing to inflict
pain upon others, she would take good care not to act
to her own discomfort. Seizing the first opportunity
that presented itself, I told Miss Stretton my determination, and, while she did not agree with me, she made
no effort to induce me to forego my resolution.

The bustle pertaining to our safe arrival at Nagasaki
drove all other subjects from my mind, and I was inclined to think that my recent troubles and quarrels

arose through the well-known activity of Satan to provide employment for idle hands. We were now busy enough. There had accumulated at Nagasaki a mass of letters and a bundle of cablegrams for Mr. Hemster which required his immediate attention, and in his disposal of these messages I caught a glimpse of the great business man he really was. However lax he might have proved in his conduct toward his only daughter, he showed himself a very Napoleon in the way he faced the problems presented to him, settling momentous affairs thousands of miles away by the dispatch of a code word or two.

In all this, so far as my abilities permitted, I was his humble assistant and I found myself filled with admiration and astonishment at his powers of concentration and the brilliancy of his methods. The little naphtha launch was kept running backward and forward between the yacht and the telegraph office, and during the long day that followed our arrival at Nagasaki that roll-top desk was a centre of commercial activity vastly different in its efficiency from the lazy routine to which I had been accustomed in the diplomatic service. My own nervous tension kept me going until the long day had passed, and the time seemed as but a few minutes. At the end I was as tired as if I had spent twelve hours continuously on the football field, and for the first time in my life I realized how men are burnt up in their pursuit of the mighty dollar. My natural inclination was to doubt whether the game was worth the candle, but during the progress of the game there was no question, for it held on the alert every faculty a man possessed, and I could well believe that it might exert a fascination that indulgence in mere gambling could never equal.

Silas K. Hemster himself was like a man transformed; the eyes which I had hitherto considered dull and uninteresting became aglow with the excitement of battle. His face was keen, stern, and relentless; I saw he was an enemy who gave no quarter and expected none. His orders to me were sharp and decisive, and I no more thought of questioning them than of offering unsought advice regarding them. He was like an exiled monarch come again to his throne; for the first time in our brief acquaintance I had seen the real Hemster, and the sight had given me a feeling of my own inane inadequacy in the scheme of things here below. When at last the day was done, his face relaxed, and he leaned back in his swivel chair, regarding me with eyes that had taken on their old kindliness. He seemed enlivened rather than exhausted by the contest, as if he had taken a sip of the elixir of youth.

"Well, my boy," he said, "you 're tired out. You look as if you had been running a race."

"That is exactly what I 've been doing, sir."

The old gentleman laughed.

"Let 's see," he mused ruminatingly, "did we have lunch or not?"

"You consumed a sandwich which I placed on your desk, Mr. Hemster, and I bolted another during one of my rushes for the dispatch-boat."

Again he laughed.

"I had forgotten," he said, "but we will enjoy our

204

dinner all the more when we sit down to it. Confess that you 're used up."

" Well, sir, I don't feel just as active as I did in the morning."

The old gentleman shook his head with a slow motion that had something of pity in it.

" You English have no aptitude for business. It shows the decadent state of Europe that Britain has held supremacy on that continent for so long."

" I should be sorry, sir, if you took me for a typical example of the English business man. I doubt if in any respect I am a credit to my country, still I am not such an idiot as to suppose I shine as a man of affairs. My training has been against me, even if I had any natural aptitude for commerce, which I doubt. Still, we are supposed to possess some creditable captains of industry on our little island."

" Supposed! That 's just it, and the supposition holds good until they are up against something better. Now, if you were in Chicago, and you wished me to join you in a deal while I was cruising on the coast of Japan, what would you do? "

" I should write you a letter explaining the project I had to put before you."

" Quite so. You would n't go to the expense of cabling the whole thing, would you? "

" If the scheme was important enough I might go to that cost."

The old gentleman held in his hand two or three cable messages which I had not seen, also a letter or two.

" Now, here is a man," he said, " who has hit upon
a plan I have often thought of myself. He has, he
tells me, made a combination which possesses considerable strength, but in order to be impregnable he
needs my co-operation. He cables the points very con-
cisely, and puts his case with a good deal of power;
but that cablegram is merely an advance agent for himself, expensive as it is. His object is to hold me at
Yokohama until he can arrive. He actually crosses
the continent to San Francisco, and takes the first
steamer for Japan. I received his cablegram at Yokohama, but did not wait for him. I sent off a word or
two myself to Chicago, asking confidential information
which I have now received. Just before we left for
Corea I got a telegram from this man in Yokohama,
asking me to wait for him at Nagasaki, which I did not
do, because I wished to impress on the energetic individual that I was not anxious to fall in with his plan,
and I knew that, having come so far, he would not return without seeing me. Meanwhile I determined to
find out whether his combination is as strong as he said
it was, and this information is now in my possession.
Also, I wished on my own account to make a combine
so formidable that whether I gave my adherence to the
one or the other my weight would tip the beam in favour of the one I joined. This combination also has
been completed, and I hold the balance, of course.
Our friend who has come over from Japan probably
does not know that there is any opposition to his
scheme, and no one in the world except yourself and
myself and a man in Chicago knows I have anything

to do with the other combine. You see I am just yachting for pleasure and for health, and am reluctant to touch business at all. At least, that is the information which I intend to be imparted to our friend, who is now impatiently awaiting me at the Nagasaki Hotel. You might think that I should invite him to come aboard my yacht and talk the matter over, or that I should go ashore and visit him, which he asks me to do; but I shall do neither. You see I want Mr. John C. Cammerford to realize that he is not nearly so important in the commercial affairs of America as he supposes himself to be."

"John C. Cammerford!" I cried in amazement. "I think I have met him in New York, though it may not be the same man."

"Well, the name is not a common one, and if you know him, all the better. I now instruct you to call on him first thing to-morrow morning. You will notice that I have trusted you fully in this matter by giving you information which must not leak through to Cammerford. You will tell him, however, that his combination is not the only one in the United States, and if I'm to join his he must prove to me that it is stronger than the opposition. He must give you a list of the firms he has combined, and he will have to show you the original documents pertaining to the options he has received. I want to know how long his options last. They will probably have at least six months' life, or he could never have taken this journey to see me. If he satisfies you that his combination is genuine, and that his options have still several months to run, then I shall

consent to meet him. If he cannot do this, or if he
refuses to do it, I shall send a few cables which will
certainly upset his apple-cart before he reaches San
Francisco. You will not promise anything on my behalf, and I should have no objection if he imagines
that my lack of eagerness in meeting him is caused by
the fact that the other combination appears to me the
stronger."

"Would you mind my sending to him your card instead of my own? He might possibly refuse to meet
me if I sent in the name of Tremorne."

"That's all right. Use my card if you wish. The
main point is that you get as much information as possible, and give as little in return as may be. There's
the dinner gong, and I'm quite ready to meet whatever's on the table. Come along."

Next morning after breakfast I went ashore, and,
arriving at the Nagasaki Hotel, sent up Mr. Hemster's
card to Mr. John C. Cammerford, and was promptly
admitted to his presence. He occupied what I took to
be the finest suite of rooms in the hotel, and had a large
table placed near the principal window of his sitting-
room, so that his back was to the light, which shone
full on the face of any visitor who called upon him. It
was quite evident to me that Mr. Cammerford hoped
to impress Silas K. Hemster with the fact that he was
carrying on great affairs right here in Japan similar to
those that occupied his attention in Chicago. The table
was littered with papers, and Cammerford sat busily
writing as if every moment was of importance. All
his plans for the impression of a visitor fell to pieces

like a house of cards when the astonished man saw
who was approaching him. He sprang to his feet with
a cry of dismay and backed toward the window. From
his position I could not very well read the expression
on his face, but it seemed to be one of fear.

" I 'm expecting another man," he cried, " you have
no right here. Get out."

" I beg your pardon, Mr. Cammerford, I have a
right here, and I have come to talk business."

" What are you following me for? Why are you
here? " he cried.

" I am here as the representative of Silas K. Hemster, of Chicago, and with his permission I sent up his
card to you."

Gradually his self-possession returned to him, but he
took care to keep the table between himself and me.
He indulged in a little cynical laugh.

" You took me by surprise, Mr. Tremorne. I—I
thought perhaps you intended trying to collect—a—
a little account of your own."

" No, I came entirely on Mr. Hemster's behalf.
Have I your permission to be seated? "

" Certainly. Sit down, sit down," and, saying this
with an effort at bluff geniality, he placed himself in
the chair he had so abruptly vacated.

" I thought, as I said before," he added, with another
uneasy laugh, " that you had some notion of collecting
a little money from me. The last time we met you held
a very mistaken view of the business matter in which
we had been associated. I assure you now — you
would n't listen then — that everything done was

strictly legal, and no one was more sorry than I that
the deal did not prove as successful as we had both
hoped."

"You cover me with confusion, Mr. Cammerford.
I have no remembrance that I ever disputed the legality
of the transaction, and I deeply regret that I seem to
have permitted myself at the time to use harsh language which you are quite justified in deploring. If
it is any comfort to you, I beg to assure you that I
look upon the half-million dollars as irretrievably lost,
and at this hour yesterday had no more idea you were
in Japan than you had that I was, if you did me the
honour to think of me."

Cammerford gazed doubtfully across the table at me,
as if he feared there was something sinister behind all
this show of submission.

"It was you, then, who sent up Mr. Hemster's
card?"

"Yes. He asked me to see you."

"Why could n't he come himself? Is he ill?"

"No, he never was in better health," I answered;
"but he is exceedingly busy. I am by way of being
his confidential man, and if you can prove to me that
the claims you have made are real, I shall have much
pleasure in arranging an interview between you."

"Oh, that 's how the land lies, is it? What do you
know of my proposals to Mr. Hemster?"

"I have read all your letters and telegrams relating
to the matter this morning; in fact, I have them in my
pocket now."

"Mr. Hemster seems to repose great trust in you.

That is rather unusual with him. I suppose you have some document to prove that you are empowered to deal?"

"As a matter of fact I am not empowered to deal. I am merely the *avant coureur* of Mr. Hemster. I sent you up his card, and here are your own letters, telegrams, and cablegrams. I was told to inform you that since you have left America another combination which Mr. Hemster considers nearly if not quite as strong as your own has been put through, and Mr. Hemster has been invited to join. He is well acquainted with the person who has effected the second combination, but, as you have just intimated, Mr. Hemster is not a man to allow personal considerations to deflect him from the strict business path. If you can show that your combination is the stronger, I can guarantee that you will have opportunity of speaking with Mr. Hemster. If not, he sails away to-morrow in his yacht, and deprives himself of the pleasure of meeting you, as you happen to be an entire stranger to him."

"How am I to show him all this if he refuses to see me?"

"You are to convince me of two things by exhibiting the original documents: first, that these firms mentioned in your letters have given you options; and second, the length of the options,—the date on which they expire, in fact."

"And if I refuse?" said Cammerford, seemingly puzzled and displeased at the trend of our conversation.

I rose to my feet and bowed to him.

"If you refuse," I said, "that ends my mission. Good-morning to you."

"Wait a bit, wait a bit," cried Cammerford, "sit down, Mr. Tremorne. This requires a little thought. Please don't go; just sit down for a moment. I don't see how Mr. Hemster can expect me to show my whole hand to one who, begging your pardon, is a comparative stranger, and one who will have nothing to do with our transaction. Secrecy is the very soul of such a deal as I am trying to put through. What guarantee have I that you will not cable to New York or Chicago full particulars of what I am asked to tell you."

"None whatever, Mr. Cammerford."

"Well, that 's not business."

"Quite so. Then I shall report your opinion to Mr. Hemster."

"What 's his object? Why does n't he come and see me himself?"

"I think I may go so far as to say that he wishes to know whether or not it is worth his while to meet you. You see, Mr. Cammerford, you are a stranger to him. He was good enough to hint that if I reported favourably on your scheme, he would wait over a day or two and go into the matter with you. As I have said, he is exceedingly busy. I left him immersed in letters and cablegrams, and all day yesterday we were over head and ears in matters of rather large importance. If you had been his Chicago acquaintance who formed the other combine, I imagine he would have seen you; as it is, he has sent me."

"Well, now, look here, Tremorne," cried Cammerford, with a fine assumption of honest bluffness, "let us talk as man to man. We 're not school-boys or sentimental girls. You know as well as I do that there is not one chance in ten million for my seeing old Hemster if the choice in the matter lies with you. You are exceedingly polite, and speak as sweetly as molasses, but I was n't born yesterday, and am not such a darned fool as to suppose you are going to put in a good word for me."

"You are quite right, Mr. Cammerford; I shall put in no good word for you that I can possibly keep out. Nevertheless I shall report fairly to Mr. Hemster exactly what you place before me."

"Oh, that 's all guff. You 'll knife me because you 've got the chance to do it. I quite admit it will be done with smooth talk, but it will be effective nevertheless."

"If you believe that, Mr. Cammerford, I shall make no endeavour to convince you of the contrary. You will act, of course, as best serves your own interest. Personally I do not care a halfpenny whether the great beef combine is formed in the interest of the dear public, or goes to smash through the non-agreement of its promoters. I fancy you cannot float such a trust and leave Mr. Hemster out, but you know more about that than I. Now it 's your next move. What are you going to do?"

Cammerford leaned across the table, showing me his crafty eyes narrowing as he seemed trying to find out what my game really was. I knew exactly where his error lay in dealing with me. He could not believe that I was honestly trying to serve my employer, and so he was bound to go wrong in any assumption formed by taking such false premises for granted.

"See here, Tremorne, I 'm going to talk straight business to you. Whatever may be our pretences, we are none of us engaged in this for our health; we want to make money. I want to make money; Hemster wants to make money; don't *you* want to make money?"

"Certainly," I replied, "that 's what I 'm here for."

"Now you 're shouting," exclaimed Cammerford, an expression of great relief coming into his face. He thought that at last he had reached firm ground. "I confess, then," he went on, "that it is supremely important I should meet Hemster, and he should be favourably disposed toward me. It is not likely I should have taken a journey clear from New York to Nagasaki if there was n't a good deal at stake. You see, I 'm perfectly frank with you. You 've got the drop on me. Just now my hands are right up toward the ceiling, and I 'm willing to do the square thing. Did you know whom you were going to meet when you left the yacht?"

"Yes, I did."

"Mr. Hemster mentioned my name to you?"

"Yes, he did."

"Did you tell him anything of our former dealings?"

"No, I did not."

"He does know you lost half a million in the States a while since?"

"Oh, yes, he knows that, but he does n't know you 're the man who got it."

"Hang it all, Tremorne; don't put it that way. I 'm not the man who got it; I lost money as well as you did."

"Oh, I beg your pardon; I thought we were talking frankly and honestly to each other. Well, be that as it may, Mr. Hemster knows I lost the money, but he does n't know you 're the man who was so unfortunate as to be in the business with me."

"Well now, Tremorne, I 'll tell you what I 'll do. You say nothing of this former company of ours, and if you will report favourably on what I have to tell you so that old Hemster will come and see me, or allow me to go to him, I 'll give you two hundred thousand dollars cash as soon as our deal is completed."

"I refuse it."

"You don't trust me?"

"No, I do not, but I refuse it nevertheless. I should refuse it if you offered me the money here and now."

Cammerford leaned back in his chair.

"You want to go the whole hog?"

"I don't know what you mean," said I.

"You want the whole five hundred thousand or nothing. Well, I tell you at once I can 't afford to give that much. I 'll raise fifty thousand dollars, and make the total amount two hundred and fifty; but I can't go a cent more, and there is no use trying to bluff me."

"I am not trying to bluff you, Mr. Cammerford. I should refuse the bribe if you made it five hundred thousand."

"Oh, it's not a bribe at all, it's—well, whatever you like to call it. Restitution if you prefer to put it that way."

"It doesn't matter what it is called, I have come for the purpose of hearing what you have to say regarding the great beef combine. If you have nothing to say I shall leave, because, as I told you, Mr. Hemster has a good deal of work on his hands, and I'm trying to help him."

"Well," said Cammerford, in a hopeless tone of voice, "you are the darndest fool I ever met in my life."

"You are not the first person who has said as much, Mr. Cammerford, although not in precisely the same language. Now, for the last time, give me a list of the names of those who are behind you."

"I'll do that if you will promise me not to say anything to old Hemster about our former relations."

"I regret that I cannot make you any such promise, Mr. Cammerford. It is my duty to lay before Mr. Hemster everything you place before me, and it is also my duty to warn him that I consider you as big a scoundrel as you consider me a fool."

"That's plain talk," said Cammerford, scowling.

"I intend it to be. Now, without further loss of time, let me see your documents."

For some minutes Cammerford maintained silence, a heavy frown on his brow, and his eyes fixed on the carpet beneath the table. At last he muttered, "Well, I'm damned!"—and, taking a bundle of papers from before him, he slipped off the elastic band, picked out one after another which he perused with care, then handed them across the table to me, watching me very narrowly as he did so. I took the papers one by one and read them over, making a note with my pencil now and then in my pocket-book. They proved to be exactly what he had said they were in his letter to Mr. Hemster. I pushed them back toward him again, saying:

"I see by some of these documents that the option is for six months, but others make no mention of the time. Why is that?"

"Because we have bought the businesses and the options are ours for ever."

"Have you anything to prove that?"

Without further reply he selected several other papers and presented them to me. These also were satisfactory.

"I shall report to Mr. Hemster that your position appears to be quite as strong as you stated it to be, and so I wish you good-morning, Mr. Cammerford."

"Hold your horses a minute," he cried, seeing me about to arise. "As you have asked me a whole lot of questions, I'd like you to answer a few of mine. Who's in this other combine?"

"I know nothing of it, except that it is in existence."

"Do you imagine it's a bluff?"

"I tell you I don't know. I should think Mr. Hemster is not a man to engage in bluff."

"Oh, isn't he? That shows how little you know of him. Have you been with him ever since he left Chicago?"

" No."

" How long have you been in his employ? "

" That is a private matter, Mr. Cammerford, which concerns no one but myself and Mr. Hemster. Besides, to tell you the truth, I came here to receive information, not to impart it; so it is useless to question me further."

" Oh, one more won't do any harm," said Cammerford, rising when I had risen; " do you think old Hemster will consent to see me? "

" I am almost certain that he will."

" Through your recommendation, eh? "

" No, I shall strongly advise him not to see you."

" Well, I 'm damned if I understand your game. It 's either too deep or too mighty shallow for me."

" It does n't occur to you, Mr. Cammerford, that there 's no game at all, and therefore there can be neither depth nor shallowness. You are troubling your mind about what does not exist."

" Then I am forced to take refuge in my former assumption, not at all a flattering one, which is that you 're a fool."

" I think that 's the safest position to assume, Mr. Cammerford; so, finally, good-bye."

I left the man standing at the head of the stairs, his hands on the banister, gazing after me with an expression of great discontent.

CHAPTER XIX

W HEN I arrived at the landing I saw the little naphtha launch making a trip from the yacht to the shore. As it swung to the steps I noticed that Gertrude Hemster was aboard with her new companion, a Japanese lady, said to be of extremely high rank, whom the girl had engaged on the first day of our arrival at Nagasaki, when her father was so deeply immersed in business. The old gentleman told me later that his daughter had taken an unfortunate dislike to Miss Stretton, and had very rapidly engaged this person, who, it was, alleged, could speak Chinese, Japanese, Corean, and pidgin English.

In spite of what her father had said, I thought the engaging of this woman with so many lingual advantages was rather a stroke aimed at myself than an action deposing Hilda Stretton. I suppose Miss Hemster thought to give proof that I was no longer necessary as interpreter on board the yacht. I doubted the accomplishments of the Japanese high dame, thinking it impossible to select such a treasure on such short notice, and so the evening before had ventured to address her in Corean; but she answered me very demurely and correctly in that language, with a little oblique smile, which showed that she knew why I had spoken to her, and I saw that I had been mistaken in slighting her educational capacities.

I went down the steps and proffered my escort to the young woman, but she was so earnestly engaged in thanking the crew of the naphtha launch that she quite ignored my presence. She sprang lightly up the steps and walked away to the nearest 'rickshaw, followed by the toddling Japanese creature. The boat's crew, who were champions of Miss Hemster to a man, each embued with intense admiration for her, as was right and natural, may or may not have noticed her contemptuous treatment of me; but after all it did not much matter, so I stepped into the launch and we set out for the yacht.

I found Mr. Hemster immersed in his papers as usual. Apparently he had never been on deck to get a breath of fresh air since his steamship arrived in the harbour.

" Well," he said shortly, looking up; " you saw Mr. Cammerford? "

" Yes."

" Did he give down or hold up? "

" He seemed very much startled when he saw me, and I had some difficulty in getting him to discuss the matter in hand."

" Was he afraid you had come to rob him, or did he think he had got me in a corner? "

" No. He knew who it was that approached him, but I should have told you, Mr. Hemster, that this is the man who got my five hundred thousand dollars some years ago, and he was under the mistaken impression that I had come to wring some part of it back from him."

"Ah, he thought you were camping on his trail, did he? What did you do?"

"I explained that I was there merely as your representative. He made some objection at first to showing his hand, as he called it; but finally, seeing that he could not come at his desired interview with you unless he took me into his confidence, he did so, although with extreme reluctance."

"Yes, and what were your conclusions?"

"My conclusions are that his letter to you was perfectly truthful. He has the following firms behind him on a six months' option, and these others have sold their businesses to him outright. His position, therefore, is all that he asserted it to be," and with this I placed my notes before my chief.

"You are thoroughly convinced of that?"

"Yes, I am; but of course you will see the papers he has to show, and may find error or fraud where I was unable to detect either."

"All right, I shall see him then."

"There is one thing further, Mr. Hemster. He offered me two hundred thousand dollars, then two hundred and fifty thousand, if I would conceal from you the fact that he had formerly defrauded me."

"Yes, and what did you say?"

"I refused the money, of course."

The old gentleman regarded me with an expression full of pity.

"I am sorry to mention it, Tremorne, but you are a numskull. Why did n't you take the money? I 'm quite able to look after myself. It does n't matter in the least to me whether or not the man has cheated everyone in the United States. If he cheats me as well, he 's entitled to all he can make. 'The laborer is worthy of his hire,' as the good Book says."

As I had used this quotation to his daughter, I now surmised that she had told her father something of our stormy conversation.

"Quite true, Mr. Hemster, but the good Book also says, 'Avoid the very appearance of evil,' and that I have done by refusing his bribe."

"Ah, well, you don't get anything for nothing in this world, and I think your duty was to have closed with his offer so long as you told me the truth about the documents I sent you to search."

"He is a man I would have nothing whatever to do with, Mr. Hemster."

"There 's where you are wrong. If he happens to possess something I want, why in the world should I not deal with him. His moral character is of no interest to me. As well refuse to buy a treatise on the English language because the bookseller drops his 'h's.' I am very much disappointed in your business capacity, Mr. Tremorne."

"I am sorry I don't come up to your expectations, sir; but he is a man whom I should view with the utmost distrust."

"Oh, if you are doing business with him, certainly. I view everyone with distrust and never squeal if I 'm cheated. Tell me about this deal with Cammerford in which you lost your money."

I related to him the circumstances of the case, which need not be set down here. When I had finished Mr. Hemster said slowly:

"If you will excuse me, Mr. Tremorne, never say that this man swindled you. Such an expression is a misuse of language. Everything done was perfectly legal."

"Oh, I know that well enough. In fact he mentioned its legality during our interview this morning. Nevertheless, he was well aware that the mine was valueless."

"What of that? It was n't his business to inform you; it was your business to find out the true worth of the mine. You are simply blaming Cammerford for your own carelessness. If Cammerford had not got the money, the next man who met you would; so I suppose he sized you up, and thought he might as well have it, and, to tell you the truth, I quite agree with him. Now, if I told you this bag contained a thousand dollars in gold, would you accept my word for it without counting the money?"

"Certainly I would."

The old gentleman seemed taken aback by this reply, and stared at me as if I were some new human specimen he had not met before.

"You would, eh?" he cried at last. "Well, you 're hopeless! I don't know but you were right to refuse his bribe. The money would not do you the least good if you got it again."

"Oh, yes, it would, Mr. Hemster. I should invest it in Government securities, and risk not a penny of it in any speculation."

"I don't believe you'd have that much sense," demurred the old gentleman, turning again to his desk. "However, you have served me well, even if you have served yourself badly. I will write a letter to Cammerford and let him know the terms on which I will join his scheme."

"You surely don't intend to do that, Mr. Hemster, without seeing the documents yourself?"

"Oh, have no fear; you must not think I am going to adopt your business tactics at my age. Run away and let Hilda give you some lunch. I shall not have time for anything but the usual sandwich. My daughter's gone ashore. She wants lunch at the Nagasaki Hotel, being tired of our ship's fare. I'll have this document ready for you to take to Cammerford after you have eaten."

Nothing loth, I hurried away in search of my dear girl, of whom I had caught only slight glimpses since her sudden dismissal by Gertrude Hemster. I was glad to know that we should have the ship practically to ourselves, and I flatter myself she was not sorry either. Lunch was not yet ready, so I easily persuaded her to come upon deck with me, and there I placed the chairs and table just as they had been at the moment when Miss Hemster had come so unexpectedly upon us.

"Now, Hilda," I began when we had seated ourselves, "I want an answer to that question."

"What question?"

"You know very well what question; the answer was just hovering on your lips when we were interrupted."

"No, it was n't."

"Hilda, there was an expression in your eyes which I had never seen before, and if your lips were about to contradict the message they sent to me——"

"Seemed to send to you," she interrupted with a smile.

"Was it only seeming, then?"

"Oh, I don't know. I 'm very much disappointed with myself. I don't call this a courtship at all. My idea of the preliminaries to a betrothal was a long friendship, many moonlight walks, and conversations about delightful topics in which both parties are interested. I pictured myself waiting eagerly under some rose-covered porch while the right person hurried toward me,—on horseback for choice. And now turn from that picture to the actuality. We have known each other only a few days; our first conversation was practically a quarrel; we have talked about finance, and poverty, and a lot of repulsive things of that sort. If I were to say, ' Yes,' I should despise myself ever after. It would appear as if I had accepted the first man who offered."

"Am I the first man, Hilda? I shall never believe it."

"I 'm not going to tell you. You ask altogether too many questions."

"Well, despite your disclaimer, I shall still insist

that the right answer was on your lips when it and you were so rudely chased away."

"Well, now, Mr. Tremorne——"

"Rupert, if you please, Hilda!"

"Well, now, Prince Rupert, to show you how far astray you may be in predicting what a woman is about to say, I shall tell you exactly what was in my mind when the thread of my thought was so suddenly cut across. There were conditions, provisos, stipulations, everything in the world except the plain and simple ' Yes ' you seemed to anticipate."

"Even in that case, Hilda, I am quite happy, because these lead to the end. It cannot be otherwise, and all the provisos and stipulations I agree to beforehand, so let us get directly to the small but important word ' Yes! ' "

"Ah, if you agreed beforehand that would not be legal. You could say you had not read the document, or something of that kind, and were not in your right mind when you signed it."

"Then let us have the conditions one by one, Hilda, if you please."

"I was going to ask you to say no more at present, but to wait until I get home. I wanted you to come to me, and ask your question then if you were still in the same mind."

"What an absurd proviso! And how long would that be? When shall you reach your own home?"

"Perhaps within a year, perhaps two years. It all depends on the duration of Mr. Hemster's voyage. Of course it is quite possible that at any minute he may make up his mind to return. I could not leave him alone here, but once he is in Chicago he will become so absorbed in business that he would never miss me."

" There is an uncertain quality about that proviso, Hilda, which I don't at all admire."

" Now, you see how it is," she answered archly; " my very first proposition is found fault with."

" On the contrary, it is at once agreed to. Proceed with the next."

" The next pertains more particularly to yourself. I suppose you have no occupation in view as yet, and I also suppose, if you think of marrying, you do not expect to lead a life of idleness."

" Far from it."

" Very well. I wish that you would offer your services to Mr. Hemster. I am sure he has great confidence in you, and as he grows older he will feel more and more the need of a friend. He has had no real friend since my father died."

" You forget about yourself, Hilda."

" Oh, I don't count; I am but a woman, and what he needs near him is a clear-headed man who will give him disinterested advice. That is a thing he cannot buy, and he knows it."

" I quite believe you, but nevertheless where is the clear-headedness? He has just asserted that I am a fool."

" He surely never called you that."

" Well, not that exactly, but as near as possible to it, and somehow, now that I am sitting opposite to you, I rather think that he is right, and I have been quixotic."

" Now I come to another condition," Hilda said with some perceptible hesitation. " It is not a condition exactly, but an explanation. I have often wondered whether I acted rightly or not in the circumstances, and perhaps your view of the case may differ from the conclusion at which I arrived. The one man with whom I should most naturally have consulted in a business difficulty—Mr. Hemster himself—was out of the question in this case, so I tried to imagine what my father would have had me do, and I acted accordingly, but not without some qualms of conscience then and since. I fear I did not do what an independent girl should have done, but now that we have become so friendly you shall be my judge."

" You will find me a very lenient one, Hilda; in fact the verdict is already given: you did exactly right whatever it was."

" Sir, you must not pronounce until you hear. We approach now the dread secret of a woman with a past. That always crops up, you know, at the critical moment. I think I told you my father and Mr. Hemster were friends from boyhood; that they went to school together; that their very differences of character made the friendship sincere and lasting. My father was a quiet, scholarly man, fond of his books, while Mr. Hemster cared nothing for literature or art, but only for an outdoor life and contest with his fellow men. It is difficult to imagine that one so sedate and self-restrained as Mr. Hemster now seems to be should have lived the life of a reckless cowboy on the plains, riding like a centaur, and shooting with an accuracy that saved his life on more than one occasion, whatever the result to his opponents. Nevertheless, in the midst of this wild career he was the first, or one of the first, to realize the future of the cattle business, and thus he laid the foundation of the colossal fortune he now possesses. I can imagine him the most capable man on the ranch, and I believe he was well paid for his services and saved his money, there being no way of spending it, for he neither drank nor gambled. While yet a very young man an opportunity came to him, and he had not quite enough capital to take advantage of it. My father made up the deficit, and, small as the amount was, Mr. Hemster has always felt an undue sense of obligation for a loan which was almost instantly repaid. When my father died he left me practically penniless so far as money was concerned, but with a musical education which would have earned me a comfortable living. Shortly after my father's death the manager of our local bank informed me that there had been deposited to my order one hundred thousand dollars' worth of stock in Mr. Hemster's great business. Now the question is, Should I have kept that, or should I have returned it to Mr. Hemster?"

"I beg your pardon, Hilda, but there is no question there at all. Your father, by reason of his most opportune loan, was quite honestly entitled to a share in the business the creation of which his money had made possible."

"But the sum given to me was out of all proportion to the amount lent. It is even more out of proportion than the figures I have mentioned would lead you to suppose, for the interest paid is so great that such an income could not be produced by four or five times the face value of the stock. Then Mr. Hemster was under no obligation to have given me a penny."

" Surely a man may be allowed to do the right thing without being legally bound to do it. I hope you accepted without hesitation."

" Yes, I accepted, but with considerable hesitation. Now, I think Mr. Hemster would be greatly annoyed if he knew I had told you all this. His own daughter has not the slightest suspicion of it, and I imagine her father would be even more disturbed if she gathered any hint of the real state of affairs. Indeed, I may tell you that she has dismissed me since this Japanese Countess came."

" Then we are in the same plight, for the young lady ordered me to resign."

" And are you going to? "

" Not likely. She did n't engage me, and therefore has no standing in the contract. But, to return to ourselves, which is always the paramount subject of interest, this dread secret, as you called it, puts an entirely different complexion on our relations. You must see that. Here have I been suing you under the impression that you were a helpless dependent. Now you turn out to be an heiress of the most pronounced transatlantic type. You once accused me of being dull in comprehension."

" I never did."

" Well, people do accuse me of that; nevertheless I am brilliant enough to perceive that this is a transformation scene, and that the dreams which I have indulged in regarding our relationship are no longer feasible."

Hilda clasped her hands and rested her elbows on the wicker table, leaning forward toward me with an expression half quizzical, half pathetic.

"I never called you dull, Mr. Tremorne——"

"Rupert, if you please."

"——but I did think you slightly original, Rupertus. Now, your talk of all this making a great difference is quite along the line of conventional melodrama. I see you are about to wave me aside. 'Rich woman, begone,' say you. You are going out into the world, registering a vow that until you can place dollar for dollar on the marriage altar you will shun me. Now I have read that sort of thing ever since I perused 'The Romance of a Poor Young Man,' but I never expected to encounter in real life this haughty, inflexible, poor young man."

"Rich woman, there are many surprises here below, and of course you cannot avoid your share of them. However, I shall not so haughtily wave you aside until you have answered that important question with a word of three letters rather than one of two. I cannot refuse what is not proffered. So will you kindly put me in a position to enact a haughty poor young man by saying definitely whether you will marry me or not?"

"I reply, 'Yes, yes, yes, yes,' and a thousand other yes's, if you wish them. Now, young man, what have you to say?"

"I have this to say, young woman, that your wealth entirely changes the situation."

"And I maintain it does n't, not a particle."

"I will show you how it does. I was poor, and I thought you were poor. Therefore it was my duty, as you remarked, to go out into the world and wring money from somebody. That, luckily, is no longer necessary. Hilda, we may be married this very day. Come, I dare you to consent."

"Oh!" she cried, dropping her hands to her side and leaning back in her creaking chair, looking critically at me with eyes almost veiled by their long lashes, a kindly smile, however, hovering about her pretty lips. "You are in a hurry, are n't you?"

"Yes, you did n't expect to clear the way so effectively when you spoke?"

Before she could reply we were interrupted by the arrival of Mr. Hemster, who carried a long sealed envelope in his hand. He gazed affectionately at the girl for a moment or two, then pinched her flushed cheek.

"Hilda, my dear," he said, "I never saw you looking exactly like this before. What have you two been talking about? Something pleasant, I suppose."

"Yes, we were," replied Hilda pertly; "we were saying what a nice man Silas K. Hemster is."

The old gentleman turned his glance toward me with something of shrewd inquiry in it.

"Hilda," he said slowly, "you must n't believe too much in nice men, young or old. They sometimes prove very disappointing. Especially do I warn you against this confidential secretary of mine. He is the most idiotically impractical person I have ever met. Would you believe it, my dear, that he was to-day offered two hundred and fifty thousand dollars if he would merely keep quiet about something he knew which he thought was his duty to tell me, and he was fool enough to refuse the good and useful cash?"

"Please tell Miss Stretton, Mr. Hemster, that the good and useful cash bore the ugly name of bribe, and tell her further that you would have refused it yourself."

"Oh, I don't know about that. I don't want the girl to think me quite in my dotage yet. Such a sum is not picked up so easily every day on the streets of Nagasaki, as I think you found out a while ago."

"It may be picked up on board a yacht," said Hilda archly, smiling up at him.

"Ah, you 're getting beyond me now. I don't know what you mean, Hilda," and he pinched her cheek again.

"And now, Mr. Tremorne, I am sorry to send you away again without lunch, but business must be attended to even if we have to subsist on sandwiches. How old a man is this Cammerford?"

"About forty, I should think."

"Does he strike you as a capable individual?"

"Naturally he does. He has proved himself to be much more capable than I am."

"Oh, that 's no recommendation. Well, I want you to take this letter to him; it is my ultimatum, and you may tell him so. He must either accept or refuse. I shall not dicker or modify my terms. If he accepts, then bring him right over to the yacht with you; if he refuses, you tell him I will have him wiped out before he can set foot in San Francisco." He handed me the sealed envelope.

"You see you were in at the beginning of this business, so I 'd like you to be on hand at the finish. I 'm sorry to make an errand-boy of you, Tremorne, but we are a little distant from the excellent messenger service of Chicago."

I rose at once, placed the envelope in my inside pocket, and said:

"I shall do my best, Mr. Hemster, although, as you have remarked, I seem to be little more than a messenger-boy in the negotiations."

"Oh, not at all; you're ambassador, that's what you are; a highly honourable position, and I feel certain that as you are not particularly fond of Cammerford your manner will go far toward showing him his own insignificance. When he once realizes how powerless he is, we 'll have no further difficulty with him."

I laughed, received a sweet smile from Hilda and a kindly nod from Hemster, then turned to the gangway and was in the ever-ready naptha launch a moment later.

Cammerford was not expecting me, so I had to search for him, and at last ran him down at the equivalent of the American bar which Nagasaki possesses for the elimination of loneliness from the children of the Spread Eagle.

"Have a drink with me, Tremorne," cried Cammerford, as genially as if we were the oldest possible friends.

234

"Thanks, no!" I replied. "I'd sooner meet the muzzle of a revolver than imbibe the alleged American drinks they furnish at this place. You see, I know the town; besides, I've come on business."

"Ah, is the old man going to see me, then?"

"That will depend on your answer to his letter which I have here in my pocket. May I suggest an adjournment to your rooms in the hotel?"

"Certainly, certainly," muttered Cammerford hastily, evidently all aquiver with excitement and anxiety.

When we reached his apartments he thrust out his hand eagerly for the letter, which I gave to him. He ripped it open on the instant, and, standing by the window, read it through to the end, then, tossing it on the table, he threw back his head and gave utterance to a peal of laughter which had an undercurrent of relief in it.

"I was to tell you," said I, as soon as I could make myself heard, "that this document is by way of being an ultimatum, and if you do not see fit to accept it——"

"Oh, that's all right, my dear boy," he cried, interrupting me. "Accept it? Of course I do, but first I must tender an abject apology to you."

"There is no necessity, Mr. Cammerford," I protested, "I hope that is not a proviso in the communication?"

"No, my dear boy, it is not. I offer the apology most sincerely on my own initiative. Actually I took you for a fool, but you are a damned sight shrewder man than I am. I told you when you were here that I could not get on to your game, but now I see it straight as a string, and I wonder I was such a chump as not to suspect it before. Tremorne, you're a genius. Of course your proper way of working was through the old man with that cursed high-bred air of honesty which you can assume better than any one I ever met. That kind of thing was bound to appeal to the old man because he's such an unmitigated rogue himself. Yes, my dear boy, you've played your cards well, and I congratulate you."

"I haven't the least idea what you are driving at," I said.

"Do you mean to tell me you don't know what is in this letter?"

"The letter was delivered to me sealed, and I have delivered it sealed to you. I have no more notion what it contains than you had before I handed it to you."

"Is that really a fact? Well, Tremorne, you're a constant puzzle and delight to me. This world would be a less interesting place if you were out of it. It is an ever-recurring problem to me whether you're deep or shallow; but if you are shallow I'll say this, that it cuts more ice than depth would do. Well, just cast your eyes over the last paragraph in that letter." He tossed across the final sheet to me, and I read as follows:

"The condition under which I shall treat with you is this: You will place at once in the Bank of Japan, to the order of Rupert Tremorne, the five hundred thousand dollars you borrowed from him, together with interest compounded for three years at six per cent. If, as is likely, you are not in a position to hand over such a sum, you may pay half the amount into the Bank of Japan here, and cable to have the other half similarly placed in the First National Bank of Chicago. The moment I receive cable advice from my confidential man of business in Chicago that the money is in the bank there, or the moment you show me the whole amount is in the bank here, I shall carry out the promises I have made in the body of this letter.

"Yours truly,

"SILAS K. HEMSTER."

The look of astonishment that doubtless came into my face must have appeared genuine to Cammerford as he watched me keenly across the table. I handed the letter back to him.

"I assure you I know nothing of this proviso."

"In that case," said Cammerford airily, "I hope you will have no objection to paying me back the money when once you have received it. I trust that your silk-stockinged idea of strict honesty will impel you toward the course I have suggested."

"I am very sorry to disappoint you, Mr. Cammerford, but circumstances have changed since I saw you last, and, if you don't mind, I'll keep the money."

Cammerford laughed heartily; he was in riotous good humour, and I suppose his compensation in this trust-forming business would be so enormous that the amount paid into the bank seemed trifling by comparison.

"I should be glad," said I, rising, "if you would pen a few words to Mr. Hemster accepting or declining his offer."

"Of course I will, dear boy," he replied, taking the latest pattern of fountain pen from his waistcoat pocket; "you are the most courteous of messengers, and I shall not keep you two shakes." Whereupon he rapidly scrawled a note, blotted it, sealed it, and handed it to me.

He arose and accompanied me to the door, placing me under some temporary inconvenience by slapping me boisterously on the shoulder.

"Tremorne, old man, you 're a brick, and a right-down deep one after all. I 'm ever so much obliged to you for lending me your money, although I did not think it would be recalled so soon, and I did not expect the interest to be so heavy. Still, I needed it at the time, and put it where it has done the most good. So long, old fellow. You will imagine yourself a rich man to-morrow."

"I imagine myself a rich man to-day, Mr. Cammerford."

CHAPTER XX

ON reaching the yacht I went directly to the old gentleman's office and handed him Cammerford's letter, which he tore open, read, and tossed on the desk.

" Mr. Hemster," said I, while an emotion which I had not suspected myself of possessing caused my voice to tremble a little; " Mr. Hemster, I don't know how I can thank you for what you have done for me to-day."

" Oh, that 's all right, that 's all right! " he said gruffly, as if the reference annoyed him. " What you need is a guardian."

" I think," said I, " I have secured one."

The old gentleman glanced up at me quickly.

" Is that so? Well, if the land lays as I have suspected, I congratulate you. Yes, and I congratulate Hilda also. As for a guardian, you have chosen a good one, and now don't begin to thank me over again, but go and tell her all about it."

Thus dismissed, I went to the saloon, and there found the lady of whom I was in search, and persuaded her to come up on deck with me. In spite of the vexatious interruption to which we had been forced to submit at this spot, I had become attached to the locality of the two chairs and the wicker table.

239

"I like this place," said I, "for its associations, and yet I am certain, the moment we begin to talk, Mr. Hemster will order me overboard, or his daughter will tell you to go down below."

"There is no immediate danger," answered Hilda. "Mr. Hemster is busy, and his daughter has not returned from Nagasaki; I suspect, however, that you should be down in the office helping your chief, rather than up here frivolously gossiping with me."

"I am obeying orders in being up here. My chief, as you call him, told me to search you out and tell you all about it."

"All about what?"

"Did you tell Mr. Hemster anything of our conversation after I left?"

"Not a word. Poor dear, his mind was occupied with other matters. He talked about you, and fished, —in, oh, such an awkward way,—to find out what I thought of you. He gave me much good counsel which I shall ever treasure, and he warned me to beware of fascinating young men, and not allow myself to become too deeply interested. Indeed I yearned to let him know that his caution was already too late; but, not being sure whether that would ease his mind or cause it greater anxiety, I held my peace. I wish you would tell him. Perhaps I should do it myself, but I cannot find the exact words, I am afraid."

"I'll tell him with great pleasure. No, to be honest, I have already told him."

"Really, and what did he say?"

"Oh, he said I needed a guardian, and I informed

him I had already secured one. He twigged the situation in a moment, congratulated me on my choice, and ordered me to come and tell you all about it."

" Tell me all about what? I 've asked you that before."

" Why, about the money with which we are to start housekeeping. Mr. Hemster estimates that it will amount to something more than half a million."

Hilda sat back in her chair with a remote resemblance to a frown on her pretty brow.

" That was what you were discussing with Mr. Hemster, was it? " she said primly.

" Of course. Don't you think it most important?"

" I suppose it is."

" He certainly thought so, and looked on me as very fortunate coming into such a tidy sum so easily."

" Easily! Did he, indeed?"

" Yes, he 's awfully pleased about it, and so am I."

" I am delighted to hear it."

" He said you would be, and he regards me as more than lucky, which, to tell the truth, I acknowledge that I am. You see it was such a complete surprise. I had n't expected anything at all, and to find myself suddenly the possessor of such a sum, all because of a few words, seemed almost too good to be true."

Hilda was leaning back in her chair; there was no question about the frown now, which was visible enough, and, as I prattled on, the displeasure in her speaking eyes became deeper and deeper.

" All because of a few words! " she murmured, as if talking to herself.

"Certainly. Plain, simple, straightforward words, yet look what an effect they had. They practically make me an independent man, even rich, as I should count riches, although I suppose Mr. Hemster would n't consider the amount very important."

"Probably not, but you seem to look upon the amount as very, very important,—even of paramount importance, I should say."

"Oh, not of paramount importance, of course, but nevertheless I shall always regard this day as the most fortunate of my life."

"Really? Because of the money, I suppose?"

"Now, Hilda," I protested, "you must admit that money is exceedingly necessary."

"I do admit it. So Mr. Hemster was more pleased about your getting the money than anything else?"

"Oh, I don't say that, but he certainly was delighted with my luck, and what true friend would n't be? I am sure my people at home will be overjoyed when they hear the news."

"Because of the money?" reiterated Hilda, with more of irritation in her tone than I had ever heard there before.

"Why not? Such a lump of gold is not won every day."

"By a few simple words," suggested Hilda tartly.

"Exactly. If you choose the psychological moment and use the right words they form a great combination, I can tell you, and success is sure to follow."

"Deserving man! I think those that called you a fool were mistaken, don't you?"

"Yes, I rather imagine they are, and in fact that has been admitted."

"So you and Mr. Hemster have been discussing this money question down in your office?"

"Yes, at first, of course. I began about the money at once, and thanked him sincerely for what he had done."

"You were quite right; if it had not been for him there would have been no money to make you so jubilant."

"That's exactly what I told him. 'Mr. Hemster,' said I, 'if it had not been for your action I should never have got a penny.'"

"Well," said Hilda, with a little break in her voice that went right to my heart and made me ashamed of myself, while the moisture gathered in her eyes, "and so you and Mr. Hemster at last got to me, and began to discuss me after the money question had been exhausted. Really, I suppose I should be thankful to have received so much attention. I wish I had known that gold occupied so large a space in your thoughts, and then I should have entered more accurately into particulars. I told you the amount was two or three times the face value of the stock, but it is what you say, over half a million, and now if you don't mind I shall go downstairs for a while."

"I do mind. I want to speak to you, Hilda."

"I would rather not talk any more just now. If you are wise you will say nothing until I have had time to think it all over."

"But I never claimed to be wise, Hilda. Sit down

243

again, I beg of you. Indeed you must, I shall not let you go at this juncture."

The flash in her eyes chased away the mist that had veiled them.

"Sir," she cried, "you are only making matters worse. If you have any care for me, say no more until I see you again."

"Hilda," said I, "I can make it all right with you in five minutes. What will you bet?"

"If you are jesting, I am tired of it. Can't you see I don't want to talk. Don't you understand you have said enough? Do be content. I wish I had n't a penny of money, and that I had never told you."

I now became aware that I was on the horns of a dilemma; I had gone too far, as a stupid man will who thinks he is on the track of a joke. The dear girl was on the verge of tears, and I saw that if I suddenly proclaimed the jest her sorrow would turn into anger against me, and my last state might be worse than my first. I had got this joke by the tail, and the whole dilemma arose through not knowing whether it was safer to hang on or let go. I quickly decided to hang on. I trusted to escape by reason of our national reputation for unreadiness, and determined to stand to my guns and proclaim that all along I had been speaking of my own fortune and not of hers. My obtuseness she would pity and forgive, but ill-timed levity and trifling with her most cherished feelings on this day of all others might produce consequences I dared not face.

"Hilda," I said, with what dignity I could bring to

my command, "you actually seem sorry at my good fortune. I assure you I expected you would rejoice with me. When I spoke to you this morning I was to all intents and purposes a penniless man, and yet, as Mr. Hemster himself informed you, I had but an hour before refused two hundred and fifty thousand dollars as a bribe. That money was but half of the fortune which this man Cammerford had previously looted from me. Now, through a few simple words in the letter Mr. Hemster wrote to him, this man is going to refund the whole half million, with interest for three years at six per cent. Therefore, my darling, imagine the delight with which I learned of this great stroke of good luck. No living person could assert here or hereafter that I was an impecunious fortune-hunter, although equally, of course, no person could have convinced you that your money weighed a particle with me when I asked you to honour me as you have done. And now, really perhaps I am too sensitive, but it seems to me that you do not take the news so kindly as I had expected."

She swayed a moment, then sank helplessly down into the armchair again.

"Rupert," she said, looking across at me with a puzzled pathos in her eyes that made me ashamed of myself; "Rupert, what are you talking about? Or am I dreaming? What half million is this you are referring to? I told you that my fortune was two or three times the hundred thousand, but I supposed you had found out its real value. Now you seem to have been speaking of something else."

" Hilda," I cried, with a horror that I hope was well simulated,—Lord forgive me for the necessity of using it,—" Hilda, you never supposed for a moment that I was referring to *your* money? "

Her troubled face seemed fixed on something intangible in the distance, as if her mind were trying to recall our conversation, that she might find some point in what I had said to account for the mistake she supposed herself to have made. The double meaning of my words was apparent enough, but of course every sentence I had uttered applied to her money equally well with my own. Now that enlightenment had come, her supposed error became obtrusively plain to her. She turned her puzzled face to me, and her expression melted into one of great tenderness as she reached forward her two hands and laid her palms on the back of mine, which rested on the wicker table.

" Rupert," she said in a low voice, " will you forgive me? I have deeply misjudged you."

" Hilda," said I, " would you have forgiven me if I had been in the wrong? "

" I would, I would, I would," she cried, and it was plain that she meant it, yet I did not dare to risk a full confession. What brutes we men are after all, and how much we stand in need of forgiveness every day of our lives!

" Tell me all about this newly found treasure," she said, and now I launched out on fresh ground once more, resolving never to get on such thin ice again after so narrow an escape. As we talked, the indefatigable little naphtha launch came alongside, and

Gertrude Hemster appeared at the gangway, followed by her miniature Countess. Miss Hemster was good enough to ignore us entirely, and, after a few words to her new companion, disappeared down the companion-way. The Countess toddled up to where we sat, and, addressing Hilda, said in her high-keyed Japanese voice:

"Mees Stretton, the mistress desires your attendance immediately," and with that she toddled away again. Hilda rose at once.

"Don't go," I commanded; but she smiled, and held out her hand to me.

"Is n't it funny," she said; "you and I together are equal to one millionaire, yet we have to dance attendance when called upon, but, unlike others in bondage, we don't need to cry, 'How long, O Lord! how long?' do we?"

"Not on your life, Hilda, as they say in the Wild West. The day of jubilee is a-coming my dear," and, in spite of her trying to slip away, I put my arm around her and drew her toward me.

"Oh, the captain is looking at us," she whispered in alarm.

"The captain is a good friend of ours, and has done the same in his time, I dare say," and with that I ——. Hilda swung herself free and fled, red as a rose. On glancing up at the bridge I noticed that the captain had suddenly turned his back on us. I always did like that rough man from Cape Cod, who would haunt the bridge during his waking hours whether the ship had steam up or not.

CHAPTER XXI

NEXT day was the most eventful I had spent on the yacht in spite of all that had gone before, for a few moments were filled with a peril which we escaped, as one might say, by a miracle, or more accurately by the prompt and energetic action of a capable man whom I shall always regard with deep affection. If Cape Cod has turned out many like him, it is a notable section of a great country.

Somewhat early in the morning I paid my third visit to the Nagasaki Hotel and brought John C. Cammerford with me to the yacht. He told me he had placed the full amount to my credit in the Bank of Japan, and said he did not need to do any cabling to America. Mr. Hemster was closeted with him in his office until the luncheon gong rang, and the amiable Cammerford was a guest at our table, referring to me several times as his old friend, and recounting stories that were more humourous than accurate about my adventures with him in the Adirondack Mountains and the fishing districts of Canada. I gathered that all the stories he had ever heard of Englishmen he now fastened on me, relating them with great gusto as having come within his own cognizance. Therefore I was delighted to be able to inform him that one of his anecdotes had appeared in

Punch in the year 1854, which he promptly denied, whereupon I proposed a modest little wager that was accepted by him under the supposition that I could not prove my assertion. But we happened to have in the library two volumes of *Punch* for that year, which I had frequently thumbed over, and I now confounded him by their production. I don't think he minded the money so much as the slight cast on what he supposed to be a genuine American joke. About three o'clock the good man left us in a high state of exultation, carried away by the useful naphtha launch.

We were all on deck about four o'clock in the afternoon when the event happened to which I have referred. Hilda and I were sitting in our chairs by the wicker table, quite boldly in the face of all, for our engagement was now public property. Gertrude Hemster and the little Japanese noblewoman were walking up and down the other side of the deck, and from the snatches of conversation wafted to us it really seemed as if Miss Hemster were learning Japanese. She had passed the ignoring phase so far as I was concerned, and had reached the stage of the icily polite and scrupulously courteous high dame, so that I quite looked forward to an intimate interview with her later on if this change continued. The old gentleman occupied his customary armchair with his feet on the rail, and it is a marvellous thing to record that during all the excitement he never shifted his position. He said afterward that it was the captain's duty to deal with the crisis, and he had absolute confidence in the captain. This confidence was not misplaced.

A CHICAGO PRINCESS

The harbor of Nagasaki is usually crowded with shipping, and steamers are continually arriving or departing, consequently they attract but little attention, for they are generally capably managed. Of course a yacht swinging at anchor with no steam up is absolutely helpless if some vessel under way bears down upon her. We were lying broadside on to Nagasaki. I was so absorbed in my conversation with Hilda that I did not notice our danger until the captain put a megaphone to his lips and vehemently hailed an oncoming steamer. Looking up, I saw a huge, black, clumsy craft steaming right down upon us, and knew in a moment that if she did not deflect her course she would cut us in two amidships. The captain, who recognized the nationality of the vessel, although I did not, roared down to me:

" What is the Chinese for ' Sheer off ? ' "

I sprang to my feet. " Fling me the megaphone," I cried. He instantly heaved it down to me, and a moment later I was roaring through it a warning to the approaching steamer. But to this not the slightest attention · was paid, nor indeed could I see anyone aboard. The black brute came on as if she were an abandoned ship without captain or crew. She appeared to grow up out of the waters; looming tremendous in size above us, and it did seem as if nothing under Heaven could save us. However, good luck and the resources of our captain did that very thing. The good luck assumed the shape of a tug which came tearing past our stern. The captain by this time was on deck with a coil of rope with a bowline on its end. Not a

" I sprang forward and caught her."

Page 251

word did he say to the flying tug, but he swung the rope so unerringly that the loop came down like a flying quoit right on the sternpost of the little vessel. In a flash the captain had the end he held twisted twice around a huge iron cleat at our side.

" Lie down, you women, at once," he roared, bracing his feet against the cleat and hanging back upon the end of the rope.

Hilda obeyed instantly, but Miss Hemster, with the Countess clinging to her, stood dazed, while I sprang forward and caught her, breaking the fall as much as was possible, all three of us coming down in a heap with myself underneath. The rope had tightened like a rod, and had either to break, jerk the tug backward out of the water, or swing us around, which latter it did, taking the yacht from under us with a suddenness that instantly overcame all equilibrium, and in a jiffy we were at right angles to our former position, while the black hulk scraped harmlessly along our side. Even now no one appeared on the deck of the Chinese steamer, but after running a hundred yards nearer the city she slowly swerved around, heading outward again, and I thought she was about to escape; but instead of that she came to a standstill a quarter of a mile or so from our position and there coolly dropped anchor.

I helped the ladies to their feet again, inquiring if they were hurt, and Miss Hemster replied with a sweet smile that, thanks to me, she was not. The Countess showed signs of hysterics with which I could not deal, therefore I turned my attention to Hilda, who by this

time had scrambled up, looking rather pale and frightened. Mr. Hemster's chair had been swung with a
crash against the bulwarks, and he had been compelled
to take his feet down from the rail, but beyond that he
kept his old position, chewing industriously at his unlit
cigar. The captain was in a ludicrously pitiable position because of a red-hot Cape Cod rage and his inability to relieve his feelings by swearing on account
of the ladies being present. Hilda noticed this and
cried with a little quivering laugh:

"Don't mind us, captain; say what you want to,
and it is quite likely we will agree with you."

The captain shook his huge fist at the big steamer
now rounding to her anchorage.

"You can say what you please," he shouted; "that
was no accident; it was intended. That damned,—
I beg your pardon, ladies,—that chap tried to run us
down, and I'll have the law of him, dod-blast-him,—
excuse me, ladies,—if there's any law in this God-
forsaken hole!"

Mr. Hemster very calmly shoved his chair back to
its former position, and put his feet once more on the
rail, then he beckoned to the captain, and when that
angry hero reached his side he said imperturbably, as
if nothing had happened:

"Captain, there's no use swearing. Besides, so
capable a man as you never needs to swear. In that
half minute you earned ten thousand dollars, and I'll
make it more if you don't think it enough."

"Nonsense," protested the captain, "it's all in the
day's work: a lucky throw of the rope, that's all."

A CHICAGO PRINCESS

"Now I see that you want to swear at somebody," Mr. Hemster went on, "and suppressed profanity is bad for the system; so I suppose you 'll prefer to swear at the person mostly to blame. Get into the launch with Mr. Tremorne here, who will translate for you, because our oaths, unlike our gold, are not current in every country. Go over to that black monstrosity; get aboard of her; find out what their game is, and swear at whoever is responsible. When we know their object we can take action, either by law, or by hiring some pirate to run her down and see how she likes it herself. I want to get at the bottom of this business."

The upshot was that the captain and I got into the naphtha launch and made directly for the Chinese steamer. We went around her twice, but saw not a soul on board, neither was there any ladder alongside by which we could ascend, or even a rope; so, after calling in vain for them to throw us a line, the captain, with an agility I should not have expected of his years and bulk, caught hold of the anchor-chain and worked himself up over the bow. His head appearing over the rail must have been a stupefying surprise to the crew, whom he found lying flat on their faces on deck. I followed the captain up the anchor-chain route, though in somewhat less effective fashion, until I was at the captain's heels. He had thrown one leg across the rail, when he whipped out a revolver and fired two rapid shots, which were followed by howls of terror. The crew had sprung to their feet and flashed out knives, but his quick revolver-shots stopped the attack even before it was rightly begun. We both leaped over the rail to the deck. The cowardly crew were huddled in a heap; no one had been killed, but two were crippled and crawled moaning on the deck; the rest had ceased their outcry and crouched together with that hopeless air of resignation to take stolidly whatever fate had in store for them, which is characteristic of the lower-class Chinese. They expected instant death and were prepared to meet it with nonchalance.

"Where is your captain?" I asked them in their own tongue.

Several of them made a motion of their head toward a low deck-house aft.

"Go and bring him," I said to one who seemed rather more intelligent than the rest. He got on his feet and went into the deck-house, presently emerging with a trembling man who admitted he was the captain.

"What did you mean," I asked him, "by trying to run us down?"

He spread out his hands with a gesture that seemed to indicate his helplessness, and maintained that it was all an accident.

"That is not true," I insisted, but nothing could budge him from his statement that the steering-gear had gone wrong and he had lost control of the ship.

"Why did n't you stop the engines when you saw where you were going?" I asked.

He had become panic-stricken, he said, and so had the crew. The engineer had run up on deck, and there was no one to shut off steam. I knew the man was lying, and told our captain so, whereupon he pressed the muzzle of his revolver against the other's forehead,

"Now question him," he said.

I did so, but the captain simply relapsed into the condition of his crew, and not another word could I get out of him.

"It's no use," I said to our captain, "these people don't mind being shot in the least. You might massacre the whole lot, and yet not get a word of truth out of any one of them previous to their extinction. Nevertheless, until you kill them they are in some wholesome fear of firearms, so if you keep the drop on the captain and his men I'll penetrate this deck-house and see what it contains."

"I would'nt do that," said our captain, "they're treacherous dogs, I imagine, and, while afraid to meet us in broad daylight on deck here, they might prove mighty handy with the knife in the darkness of that shanty. No, send the captain in and order him to bring out all his officers, if he's got any."

This seemed practical advice, so, asking our captain to remove his revolver from the other's forehead, I said to the latter:

"How many officers have you?"

He answered that there were five.

"Very well, go and bring them all out on deck here."

He gave the order to one of the crew, who went into the deck-house and presently came out with five discouraged-looking Chinese ship's officers. There was nothing to be made out of this lot; they simply stood in a row and glowered at us without answering. Whenever I put a question to them they glanced at the captain, then turned their bovine gaze upon me, but never once did one of them open his mouth.

" Now, captain," said I, " I propose that we herd this whole mob, officers and men, into the forecastle. The windlass, anchor-tackle, and all that will impede them, if they endeavour to take concerted action. You stand here on the clear deck with your two revolvers and keep an eye on them. The captain and officers will probably imagine you understand Chinese, too, so they will give no orders. Then I shall penetrate into the deck-house, for I am convinced that we have not yet come upon the responsible man. I don't believe this fellow is the captain at all."

To all this my comrade agreed, although he still demurred at my entering the deck-house. I ordered the men forward and then lined the alleged captain and his officers along the rail near them, and, while my captain stood by with a revolver in each hand, I, similarly equipped, went down three steps into the low cabin. It was a dangerous move if there had been anyone of courage within, for there were no windows, and what little light penetrated the place came in through the open door, and that was now largely shut out by the bulk of my body. Knowing that I was rather conspicuously silhouetted against the outside glare and formed an easy mark for either pistol or knife, I stepped down as quickly as possible and then stood aside. I thought at first the place was empty, but as my eyes became accustomed to the gloom I saw that a bench ran around three walls and in the further corner was a huddled figure which I knew.

"Ah, Excellency Hun Woe!" I cried, covering him with the revolver, "it is to you then we were to have been indebted for our death."

The wretch flung himself on his face at my feet, moaning for mercy. A Corean never has the nonchalance of a Chinaman when danger confronts him.

"Get up from the floor and sit down where you were," I said; "I want to have some conversation with you." Then I went to the door again and cried to the captain:

"It 's all right. There is no one here but the Prime Minister of Corea, and I think I begin to see daylight so far as this so-called accident is concerned. I want to have a few minutes' talk with him, so, unless you hear a pistol-shot, everything is going well."

"Good enough," cried the genial captain, "you play a lone hand for all it 's worth, and I 'll hold up these hoodlums while you pow-wow."

"Now, Hun Woe," I cried, turning to him, "what is the meaning of this dastardly trick?"

"Oh, Excellency," he moaned, "I am the most miserable of men."

"Yes, you are. I admit that, and, furthermore, unless you tell the truth you are in some danger of your life at this moment."

"My life," he went on,—and I knew he spoke truly enough,—"is already forfeited. My family and my kinsmen are all in the hands of the Emperor. Their heads will fall if I do not bring back the white woman whom the Emperor has chosen for his mate."

"But how in Heaven's name would it have brought

257

back the white woman if you had run us down and drowned us all?"

"We have expert swimmers aboard," he said, "divers brought for the purpose, who would have saved the white woman, and indeed," he added hurriedly, "would have saved you all, but the white woman we would have brought back with us."

"What a hairbrained scheme!" I cried.

"Yes, Excellency, it is not mine. I but do what I am ordered to do. The Emperor wished to sink the war-vessel of the American King so that he might not invade our coasts."

"Is it true that the Empress has been murdered?"

"Ah, not murdered, Excellency; she died of a fever."

"She looked anything but feverish when I saw her the day before," I insisted.

"We are all in God's hands," said the Prime Minister with a shrug of resignation, "and death sometimes comes suddenly."

"It does indeed in Seoul," I commented, whereupon the Prime Minister groaned aloud, thinking probably of his own impending fate and that of his wife, children, and kinsfolk.

"Excellency," he went on with the courage of desperation, "it is all your fault. If you had not brought that creature to Seoul, I would have been a happy man to-day. I have always been your friend, and it is said your country stands by its friends; but that, I fear, is not true. You can help me now, but perhaps you will not do it."

"I admit it is largely my fault, although, like yourself, I was merely the Prime Minister on our side of the affair. Nevertheless, if there is anything I can do to help you, Hun Woe, I shall be very glad to do it."

He brightened up perceptibly at this, and said eagerly, as if to give further spur to my inclination:

"If you do, I will make you a rich man, Excellency."

Nothing showed the desperate nature of his case more conclusively than this offer of money, which is always a Corean's very last card.

"I do not want a single sek from you, Hun Woe; in fact I am willing to give away many thousands of them if it will aid you. Tell me what I can do for you. I will even go so far as to return with you to Seoul and beg or bribe the Emperor's clemency."

"That would indeed be useless," demurred the Prime Minister; 'His Majesty would promise you anything and take what money you liked to give him; but my body would be dismembered as soon as you were gone, and all my kinsfolk killed or sent to slavery."

I knew this to be an accurate presentation of the case.

"What, then, can I do for you?" I asked.

He lowered his voice, his little eyes glittering.

"There is but one thing to do, and that is to get the white woman on board this ship."

"To kidnap her? That is impossible; you cannot do it here in Japan, and you could not do it even if the ship were lying in Chemulpo roadstead. It is a dream of foolishness, and if your Emperor had any sense he would know it could not be done."

"Then," wailed Hun Woe, "my line is extinguished, and the deaths of myself and of my relatives lie at your door, who brought the accursed white woman to Seoul."

His lamentations disturbed me deeply, because, for a wonder, he spoke the truth.

"I 'll tell you what I will do, Hun Woe, which will be far more effective than your ridiculous project of kidnapping the young lady. Has not your Emperor the sense to see, or have you not the courage to tell him, that if you succeeded in getting Miss Hemster to Seoul you would bring down on yourselves the whole force of America, and probably of England as well? Either country could blot Seoul, Palace and all, off the face of the earth within half an hour of surrounding it, and they would do it, too, if needs be. You know I speak the truth; why did you not explain this to the Emperor?"

"His Majesty would not believe me; his Majesty cares for nothing but the white woman; so any other plan but that of getting her is useless."

"No, it is n't. So far as you are concerned, Hun Woe, it would be useless for me to appeal to either the English or the American authorities. They will never interfere unless one of their own citizens is in jeopardy, but I can trust the Japanese. I am sure Mr. Hemster will lend me his yacht, and I will take a party of fearless Japanese with me to the capital and to the Palace. There will be no trouble. I shall return with your

family and your kinsmen, escort them down to Chemulpo, and I shall deliver them to you here in Nagasaki. So long as you remain in Nagasaki you are
safe."

This brave offer brought no consolation to the Prime
Minister of Corea: he shook his head dolefully, and
told me what I already knew, that a man who fled from
Corea to Nagasaki had been nearly murdered here by
Coreans, then, thinking himself more safe under the
British flag, he had escaped to Shanghai, where he was
followed and killed in cold blood, his mutilated remains
being taken to Seoul, and there exhibited. All his
relatives and his family had already preceded him into
the unknown.

"Nothing will suffice," groaned the Prime Minister,
"but the white woman,— may curses alight on her
head!"

"Do not be so downhearted; my scheme is quite
practicable, while yours is not. Mr. Hemster is the
most generous of men, and I am certain he will see you
and your family safe across the Pacific to the United
States, and there I will guarantee no Corean will ever
follow you. You have money enough if you can get
your hands on it. Perhaps you have some here with
you now."

"Yes," he replied simply, "I have my whole fortune
on board this ship."

"There you are. I see you did not intend to return
to Corea if you could not get the white woman."

"It was not that. I brought my fortune to give it
away in bribes."

" And that 's why you offered me a bribe ? "

" Yes, Excellency," he replied with childlike candour.

" Well, Hun Woe, take my advice. I think I shall be able to get you all clear away. You are in command here, and these Chinese would rather die than split on you, so perhaps, instead of taking Mr. Hemster's yacht, we had better stick to this vessel, and I will bring my band of Japanese aboard. However, keep up your courage until I have seen Mr. Hemster, and then I will let you know what I am prepared to do. As this ship is now empty you had better spend your time and money in Nagasaki filling her with coal. We will go to Corea, get your family and relatives aboard, and then you can sail direct for San Francisco. It is a wild project, but with a little courage I make no doubt it can be carried out, and if you have n't money enough I can help you. Indeed, now that I have considered the matter, I shall not ask Mr. Hemster for his yacht at all. This ship is the very thing. All you need is plenty of coal and plenty of provisions, and these you can get at Nagasaki without attracting the least attention. Mr. Hemster could not accommodate you all on his yacht even if he consented to do so. Yes, cheer up, my plan is quite feasible, while yours is impossible of execution. You can no more get the girl than you can get the moon for the Emperor of Corea."

So, telling the Prime Minister that I would call upon him next day and discuss particulars, I left him there, asked the captain to release the patient crew and their officers, threw a rope ladder down the side, and so descended to our waiting naphtha launch, the crew of which had been rather anxious at the long silence following the two rapid shots; but they had obeyed orders and stood by without attempting to board.

CHAPTER XXII

SILAS HEMSTER was sitting in his wicker chair on deck just as I had left him, so I drew up another chair beside him and sat down to give him my report. He listened to the end without comment.

"What a darned-fool scheme," he said at last. "There was n't one chance in a thousand of those chumps picking any of us out alive if they had once destroyed the yacht. Do you think they will attempt it again?"

"Well, it seems as if I had discouraged old Hun Woe, but a person never can tell how the Oriental mind works. He stated that the precious plan emanated from the Emperor, who wished at a blow to destroy your fleet, as it were, and capture your daughter; but it is more than likely the scheme was concocted in his own brain. He is just silly enough to have contrived it, but I rather imagine our good captain overawed the officers and crew to such an extent that they may be chary of attempting such an outrage again. When two of us had no difficulty in holding up the whole company, they may fear an attack from our entire crew. Still, as I have said, no one can tell what these people will do or not do. The Prime Minister himself, of course, is in a bad way, and I should like to enable him to escape if I could."

"You intend, then, to carry out the project you outlined to him?"

"I certainly do, with your permission."

"Well, not to flatter you, Tremorne, I think your invasion of Corea at the head of a band of Japanese is quite as foolhardy as his attempt to run down the yacht."

"Oh, no, Mr. Hemster; the Coreans are a bad people to run away from, but if you face them boldly you get what you want. They call it the Hermit Kingdom, but I should call it the Coward Kingdom. A squad of determined little Japs would put the whole country to flight."

"Well, you can do as you like, and I'll help you all I'm able. Of course you're not responsible for the plight of the Prime Minister; I'm the cause of the mix-up, and if you want the yacht you just take it, and I'll stay here in Nagasaki with the womenfolk till you return; but if I had my way I'd clear out of this section of the country altogether."

"Why not do so, Mr. Hemster. I have entirely given up the notion of taking the yacht, because the Chinese steamer will be much less conspicuous and will cause less talk in Chemulpo than the coming back of the yacht. Of course the Emperor will have spies down at the port, and it will seem to them perfectly natural for the black ship to return. Meanwhile, before his Majesty knows what has happened, I shall be up in Seoul and in the Palace with my Japanese, and I think I shall succeed in terrorizing the old boy to such an extent that in less than ten minutes we shall be

marching back again with Hun Woe's whole family
and troop of relatives. 'Once aboard the lugger' they
are safe, for Corea has no ship to overtake them, and
the whole thing will be done so suddenly that the Chinese steamer will be half-way across the Pacific, or the
whole way to Shanghai, before the Coreans have made
up their minds what to do. I shall leave with the
ship, and have them drop me at Nagasaki or Shanghai,
or whatever port we conclude to make for. Then I
can rejoin the yacht at any port we agree upon."

"You appear to think you 'll have no trouble with
your expedition, then?"

"Oh, not the slightest."

"Well, you know, we had trouble enough with
ours."

"Yes, but this is a mere dash of twenty-six miles
there and twenty-six miles back. We ought to be able
to do it within a day and a night, and if old Hun Woe
attends rightly to his coaling and his provisioning, all
Corea cannot stop him. I think he is badly enough
frightened not to omit any details that make for his
safety."

"Very well, we 'll stay right here till you return. I
suppose that old Chinese tub will take some time worrying her way to Corea and back again, although I 'll
confess she seemed to come on like a prairie fire when
she was heading for us. Now I guess everybody is
just a little tired of life on shipboard. I 've noticed
that when a lot of people are cooped up together for a
while things don't run on as smoothly as they might
sometimes, so I 'll hire a floor in the principal hotel

here and live ashore until we see your Chinese steamer come into the harbour again. I suppose the captain will prefer to live on the yacht, but the rest of us will sample hotel life. I 'm rather yearning for a change myself; besides I think my daughter would be safer ashore than on board here, for one can't tell, as you said, what these hoodlums may attempt; and as long as they 're convinced she 's on the yacht we 're in constant danger of being run down, or torpedoed, or something. Now, you would n't mind telling my daughter what you 've told me about the intentions of this here Prime Minister? She 's rather fond of wandering around town alone, and I guess she 'd better know that until this Chinese steamer sails away she is in some danger."

" I suggest that she should n't go sightseeing or shopping without an escort, Mr. Hemster."

" Well, a good deal will depend on what Gertie thinks herself, as perhaps you have found out while you 've been with us."

He sent for his daughter, and I placed a third chair for the girl when she arrived. She listened with great interest to my narration of the events on board the Chinese steamer, and I added my warning that it was advisable for her not to desert the frequented parts of Nagasaki, and never to make any expedition through the town without one or more masculine persons to protect her. She tossed her head as I said this, and replied rather cuttingly:

" I guess I 'm able to take care of myself."

I should have had sense enough to let it go at that, but I was much better aware of her peril then even her

father was, for I knew Nagasaki like a well-thumbed
book; so I said it was a regular labyrinth into whose
mazes even a person intimately acquainted with the
town might get lost, and as the Prime Minister had
plenty of money at his command, he had the choice of
all the outscourings of the nations here along the port,
who would murder or kidnap without a qualm for a
very small sum of ready cash.

"There is no use in saying anything more, Mr. Tremorne," put in her father, definitely; "I'll see to it
that my daughter does not go abroad unprotected."

"Well, Poppa," she cried, "I like the hotel idea first
rate, and I'm going there right away; but I want a
suite of rooms to myself. I'm not coming down to the
public table, and I wish to have the Countess and my
own maid with me and no one else."

"That's all right," said her father, "you can have
what you like. I'll buy the whole hotel for you if you
want it."

"No, I just wish a suite of rooms that will be my
own; and I won't have any visitors that I don't invite
specially."

"Won't you allow me to visit you, Gertie?" asked
the old gentleman with a quizzical smile.

"No, I don't want you or any one else. I'm just
tired of people, that's what I am. I intended to propose going to the hotel anyhow. I'm just sick of this
yacht, and have a notion to go home in one of the regular steamers. I'm going right over to the hotel now
and pick my own rooms."

"Just as you please," concurred her father. "Per-

haps Mr. Tremorne will be good enough to escort you
there."

" I have told you that I don't want Mr. Tremorne,
or Mr. Hemster, or Mr. Anybody-else. If I must have
an escort I 'll take two of the sailors."

" That will be perfectly satisfactory. Take as many
trunks as you want, and secure the best rooms in the
hotel."

Shortly afterward Miss Hemster, with her maid
and the Countess, left the yacht in the launch, the
mountain of luggage following in another boat. The
launch and the boat remained an unconscionably long
time at the landing, until even Mr. Hemster became
impatient, ordering the captain to signal their return.
When, in response to this, they came back, the officer
in charge of the launch told Mr. Hemster that his
daughter had ordered them to remain until she sent
them word whether or not she had secured rooms to
her satisfaction at the hotel. Meanwhile she had given
the officer a letter to her father, which he now handed
to the old gentleman. He read it through two or three
times with a puzzled expression on his face, then
handed it to me, saying:

" What do you make of that? "

The letter ran as follows:

" DEAR POPPA:

" I have changed my mind about the hotel, and, not
wanting a fuss, said nothing to you before I left. As I told
you, I am tired to death of both the yacht and the sea, and I
want to get to some place where I need look on neither of
them. The Countess, who knows more about Japan than Mr.

Tremorne thinks he knows, has been kind enough to offer me
her country house for a week or two, which is situated eight
or nine miles from Nagasaki. I want to see something of high
life in Japan, and so may stay perhaps for two weeks; and it
you are really as anxious about my kidnapping as you pretend,
you may be quite sure I am safe where I am going,— much
more so than if I had stayed at the hotel at Nagasaki. I don't
believe there's any danger at all, but think Mr. Tremorne
wants to impress you with a feeling of his great usefulness,
and you may tell him I said so if you like. Perhaps I shall tire
of the place where I am going in two or three days; it is more
than likely. Anyhow, I want to get away from present company for a time at least. I will send a message to you when I
am returning.

"Yours affectionately,

"GERTIE."

This struck me as a most ungracious and heartless
communication to a father who was devoting his life
and fortune to her service. I glanced up at the old
gentleman; but, although he had asked my opinion on
this epistle, his face showed no perturbation regarding
its contents. I suppose he was accustomed to the
young woman's vagaries.

The letter seemed to me very disquieting. It had
been written on board the yacht before she left, so
perhaps the country house visit had been in her mind
for some time; nevertheless there were two or three
circumstances which seemed to me suspicious. It was
an extraordinary thing that a Countess should take
what was practically a servant's position if she possessed a country house. Then, again, it was no less
extraordinary that this Japanese woman should be able
to speak Corean, of which fact I had had auricular

demonstration. Could it be possible that there **was**
any connection between the engaging of this woman
and the arrival of the Chinese steamer? Was the so-
called Countess an emissary of the Corean Prime Minister? A moment's reflection caused me to dismiss
this conjecture as impossible, because Miss Hemster
had engaged the Countess on the day she arrived at
Nagasaki, and, as our yacht was more speedy than any
other vessel that might have come from Corea, all idea
of collusion between the Corean man and the Japanese
woman seemed far fetched. Should I then communicate my doubts to Mr. Hemster? He seemed quite at
his ease about the matter, and I did not wish to disturb
him unnecessarily. Yet he had handed me the letter,
and he wished my opinion on it. He interrupted my
meditations by repeating his question:

"Well, what do you make of it?"

"It seems to me the letter of one who is accustomed
to think and act for herself, without any undue regard
to the convenience of others."

"Yes, that 's about the size of it."

"Has she ever done anything like this before?"

"Oh, bless you, often. I have known her to leave
Chicago for New York and turn up at Omaha."

"Then you are not in any way alarmed by the receipt of this?"

"No, I see no reason for alarm; do you?"

"Who is this Countess that owns the country
house?"

"I don't even know her name. Gertie went ashore
soon after we came into the harbour and visited the

American Consul, who sent out for this woman, and Gertie engaged her then and there."

"Is n't it a little remarkable that she speaks Corean?"

"Well, the American Consul said there was n't many of them could; but Gertie, after being at Seoul, determined to learn the language, and that's why she took on the Countess."

"Oh, I see. She stipulated, then, for one who knew Corean?"

"Quite so; she told me before we left Chemulpo that she intended to learn the language."

"Well, Mr. Hemster, what you say relieves my mind a good deal. If she got the woman on the recommendation of the American Consul, everything is all right. The coming of the Prime Minister, and the fact that this Countess understands Corean, made me fear that there might be some collusion between the two."

"That is impossible," said Mr. Hemster calmly. "If the Corean Minister had come a day or two before the Countess was engaged, there might have been a possibility of a conspiracy between them; but convincing proof that such is not the case lies in the fact that the Prime Minister would not then have needed to run us down, which he certainly tried to do."

I had not thought of this, and it was quite convincing, taken in the light of the fact that Miss Hemster had frequently acted in this impulsive way before.

We resolved not to leave the yacht that night, even if we left it at all, now that Miss Hemster had taken herself into the interior. Whatever she thought, or whatever her preferences were, I imagine her father liked the yacht better than a hotel.

Hilda and I went on deck after dinner and remained there while the lights came out all over Nagasaki, forming a picture like fairyland or the superb setting of a gigantic opera. We were aroused by a cry from one of the sailors, and then a shout from the bridge.

" That Chinese beast is coming at us again ! "

Sure enough the steamer had left her moorings, rounded inside toward the city, and now was making directly toward us without a light showing.

" Get into the boats at once," roared the captain.

I hailed Hemster, who was below, at the top of my voice, and he replied when I shouted : " Come up immediately and get into the small boat."

By the time he was on deck I had Hilda in one of the boats, and Mr. Hemster was beside her a moment later. Two sailors seized the oars and pushed off. The next instant there was a crash, and the huge black bulk of the Chinese steamer loomed over us, passing quickly away into the night. I thought I heard a woman scream somewhere, but could not be quite sure.

" Did you hear anything ? " I asked Hemster.

" I heard an almighty crashing of timber. I wonder if they 've sunk the yacht."

The captain's gruff voice hailed us.

" They 've carried away the rudder," he said, " and shattered the stern, but not seriously. She will remain afloat, but will have to go into dry-dock to-morrow."

CHAPTER XXIII

THE Chinese steamer, if indeed it were she, although we could not be sure in the darkness, had sent us to the hotel when we had made up our minds not to go. We in the boat hovered near the yacht long enough for the captain to make a hurried examination of the damage. The wreck certainly looked serious, for the overhang of the stern had been smashed into matchwood, while the derelict rudder hung in chains like an executed pirate of a couple of centuries agone. It was impossible at the moment to estimate with any degree of accuracy the extent of the disaster. The captain reported that she was not leaking, and therefore her owner need have no fear that she would sink during the night. The rudder had certainly been carried away, and probably one of the propellers was damaged. In any case the yacht would have to go into dry-dock; so, being satisfied on the score of immediate safety, Mr. Hemster gave orders to pull ashore, and thus we became guests of the Nagasaki Hotel.

Next morning the Chinese steamer was nowhere in sight, so it was reasonably certain she had been the cause of our misfortune. The yacht rode at its anchorage, apparently none the worse so far as could be seen from the town. Before noon the craft was in dock, and we learned to our relief that her propellers were untouched. She needed a new rudder, and the rest was mere carpenter work which would be speedily accomplished by the deft Japanese workmen. Mr. Hemster had his desk removed to a room in the hotel, and business went on as before, for there were still many details to be settled with Mr. John C. Cammerford before he proceeded toward San Francisco. I think we all enjoyed the enlarged freedom of residence on shore, and the old gentleman said that he quite understood his daughter's desire to get away from sight of sea or ship. It struck me as remarkable that he was not in the slightest degree alarmed for the safety of his daughter, nor did he doubt for a moment her assertion that she was going to stop at the country house of the Countess. On the other hand I was almost convinced she had been kidnapped, but did not venture to display my suspicions to her father, as there seemed no useful purpose to be served by arousing anxiety when my fears rested purely on conjecture. Of course I consulted confidentially with Hilda, but a curious transformation had taken place in our several beliefs. When she spoke of the probability of the girl's committing suicide or doing something desperate, I had pooh-poohed her theory. We had each convinced the other, and I had adopted her former view while she had adopted mine. She had heard no scream on the night of the disaster, and regarded it as a trick of my imagination.

But what made me more uneasy was the departure of the Prime Minister. His fears for himself and family were genuine enough, and he was not likely to abandon a quest merely because his first effort had failed. It meant death to him if he returned to Seoul without the girl, so, if he had not captured her, it seemed incredible that he should return the same night without a single effort to accomplish his mission. The second,—and, as far as he knew, successful,—essay to sink the yacht, must have been to prevent pursuit. He was probably well aware that the yacht was the fastest steamer in the harbour, and, if it were not disabled, would speedily overhaul him. He also knew that his officers and crew were no heroes, and that with half-a-dozen energetic Japanese in addition to our own crew we could capture his steamer on the high seas without the slightest effort being put forth to hinder us. He had now a clear run to Chemulpo, and, however resolute we were, there was no possibility of our overtaking him. I had offered him my assistance, which he had accepted in a provisional sort of way, yet here he had disappeared from the scene without leaving word for me, and apparently had returned to the land where his fate was certain if he was unsuccessful. Of course, he might have made for Yokohama or Shanghai, but I was convinced, after all, that he cared more for the safety of his family than for his own, and indeed, if he was thinking only of himself, he was as safe in Nagasaki as elsewhere. I could therefore come to no other conclusion than that the girl was aboard the Chinese steamer and was now a prisoner on her way to Seoul, but of this I could not convince Hilda Stretton, and Mr. Hemster evidently had no misgivings in the matter.

A CHICAGO PRINCESS

Obviously the first thing to do was to learn the antecedents of the so-called Japanese Countess, and with this intent I called at the American Consulate. The official in charge received me with the gracious goodcomradeship of his nation, and replied with the utmost frankness to my questions. He remembered Miss Hemster's visit of a few days before, and he assured me that the Countess was above suspicion. As for her knowledge of Corean, that was easily accounted for, because her late husband had been a Japanese official at Seoul a dozen years or so ago, and she had lived with him in that city. Corea, indeed, had been in a way the cause of the Countess's financial misfortunes. Her husband, some years before he died, had invested largely in Corean enterprises, all of which had failed, and so left his wife with scarcely anything to live upon except the country house, which was so remote from Nagaski as to be unsalable for anything like the money he had expended upon it. Exactly where this country house was situated the United States Consul professed himself ignorant, but said he would endeavour to find out for me, and so genially asked me to take a drink with him and call a few days later.

This conversation did much to dissipate my doubts. Of course, without Mr. Hemster's permission I could not tell the Consul the full particulars of the case, or even make any reference to them. So far as that courteous official knew, I was merely making inquiries on behalf of Mr. Hemster about the woman engaged to be his daughter's companion, and about the country house which the girl had been invited to visit. The

277

Consul assured me that everything was right and proper, and that Miss Hemster would get a glimpse of the inner life of the Japanese not usually unfolded to strangers, and thus my reason was convinced, although my instinct told me there was something unaccountable in all this. The scream I had heard simultaneously with the crashing of the collision might of course have been the shrill shriek of one of the Chinese sailors, but at the time it had sounded to me suspiciously like the terrified exclamation of a woman. Then, again, the action of the Prime Minister remained as unaccountable as ever, unless my former theory proved correct. However, I got the name of the Countess, which none of us who remained had known before, and I promised to return and learn the situation of the country house. My visit, on the whole, was rather reassuring; for, after all, there was little use in attaching too much importance to the actions of any Corean, even though he were Prime Minister of that country; so the problem began to appear to be a self-conjured one, and I gradually came to recognize that I had been troubling myself for nothing.

The week that followed was one of the most delightful in my existence. The captain was superintending the repairs on the yacht, and the intricacies of Mr. Hemster's business activity were such that I could not be of much assistance to him; so there was practically nothing to do but to make myself agreeable to that dear girl, Hilda, to whom I showed whatever beauties Nagasaki possessed, and surely no one knew the town better than I did. She took a vivid interest, not only in the place, but also in my own somewhat doleful experience there in former and less happy times, not yet remote, the recital of which experiences rendered the present all the more glorious by contrast.

On our tenth day ashore Hilda told me that the old gentleman was beginning to worry because he had heard nothing from his daughter, and Hilda herself expressed some uneasiness because of the long silence. This aroused all my old doubts, and I called a second time on the American Consul. He told me that the information I sought had been in hand several days. The villa was called " The House of the Million Blossoms," and it was situated nearly ten miles from Nagasaki. He produced a sketch map, drawn by himself, which he said would guide me to the place, so I resolved to visit it without saying a word to anyone.

I found the villa of the Blossoms without the least difficulty, and a most enchanting spot it appeared to be. Situated inland, at the bottom of a sheltered valley, through which ran a trickling stream, the place had evidently been one of importance in its day; but now the entrance lodge showed signs of dilapidation, and the plantation itself was so marvellously overgrown as to be almost a wilderness, with foliage too thick for me to see anything of the house itself. The custodian of the lodge received me with great urbanity but no less firmness. He confessed that the ladies were there, but added that he had strict orders to allow no one to enter or even to approach the house. I asked him to take my card to the stranger lady, and, although at first he demurred, I overcome his reluctance by an urbanity which I flatter myself was a stage imitation of his own, and, what was more to the purpose, I induced him to accept a present in the coinage of the realm. Nevertheless he securely barred the gate and left me outside, showing that his trust in my good faith was either very weak, or that his politeness was confined to the flowery language of his country. After a long absence he returned, and handed to me a folded sheet of note paper which I recognized as belonging to the stationery of the yacht. It bore these words in English, and in Miss Hemster's handwriting:

"I wish to remain here in seclusion, and I consider it very impertinent of you to have sought me out. I am perfectly happy here, which I was not on board the yacht, and all I wish is to be left alone. When good and ready I will write to the yacht and to the Nagasaki Hotel. Until that time it is useless for you to intrude."

This was definite enough, and I turned away angry with myself for having played the busybody, not knowing enough to attend to my own affairs. I had intended to tell the young woman of the accident to the yacht, making that in some way the excuse for my visit; but in the face of such a message I forgot all about the information I desired to impart, and so returned in a huff to Nagasaki. This message set at rest all thoughts of kidnapping, although it left my honoured friend Hun Woe's precipitate departure as much a mystery as ever.

On my arrival at the hotel I showed the note to Hilda, who averred there could be no doubt about its genuineness, and she asked my permission to give it to

Mr. Hemster to allay his rapidly arising anxiety, which mission it certainly performed as completely as it had snubbed me.

Next day the yacht was floated and appeared none the worse for the collision. The captain took her out to the anchorage, and so we waited several days to hear from the girl, but no word came. Finally her father wrote a letter to her, beseeching some indication of her plans, and this was sent by messenger to the House of the Million Blossoms. The old gentleman had become exceedingly tired of Nagasaki, and very evidently did not know what to do with himself. The messenger returned, but brought no answer. He said the man at the gate had taken in the letter, and brought out the verbal message that the lady would write when she was ready to do so. This was the reverse of satisfactory, and Mr. Hemster roamed about disconsolately like a lost spirit. Hilda said he told her that his daughter had never before remained in the same mind for two days together, and this prolonged country-house visit caused him great uneasiness. He now became infused with the kidnapping idea, not fearing that she had been taken away to Corea, but believing that the Japanese were holding her prisoner, perhaps with the idea of a ransom later on. Finally Mr. Hemster determined to visit the House of the Million Blossoms himself, and he insisted on Hilda's accompanying us, which she did with some reluctance. Never did she believe that this was other than one of the girl's prolonged caprices to make us all anxious, hoping to laugh at us later on for being so.

At the gateway we were met by the same imperturbable guardian, who was as obdurate as ever. He would take in any message, he said, but would not permit us to enter even the grounds. Mr. Hemster sent a letter he had written at the hotel, and in due time the keeper came out with a signed note, somewhat similar to the one I had received. It said:

" DEAR FATHER :
" Do not worry about me; I am perfectly happy and wish to remain here a few days longer.
"Your affectionate daughter,
" G."

After reading this he passed it on to Hilda and me in silence. He got into his 'rickshaw without a word, and we entered ours. The men tottered along until we were out of sight of the lodge, and then Mr. Hemster called a halt. He sprang out, and, approaching me, said :

" Well, Tremorne, what do you make of it ? "

The voice in which his question was put quivered with anguish, and, glancing at his face, I saw it drawn and haggard with an expression that betokened terror.

" Oh, there 's nothing to make of it, Mr. Hemster, except that the young lady, for some reason unknown to me, desires to make you anxious and has succeeded."

" Tremorne," he said, unheeding this attempted consolation, " look at this note. It was not written to-day, but weeks ago. It was written on board the yacht, and so was the one you received, although I did not notice that at the time. This was written with a stub pen, the same that she used in sending me the first letter; but this pen she did not take away with her, nor the ink. My poor girl has been deluded into writing those letters by some one who had a subtle end to serve. I cannot fathom the mystery, but I am certain she is not in that house."

I sprang down from my 'rickshaw.

" I 'll soon settle that point," I cried, " I will crush through the boundary hedge, and break in the door of the house. If there are any ladies within they will soon make an outcry, which will reveal their presence. You wait for me here."

To this he at once agreed, and with some difficulty I got into the thick plantation, through which I made my way until I came to the house, the first look at which convinced me it was empty. There is something of desolate loneliness about a deserted house which instantly strikes a beholder.

There was no need for me to break in, for one of the windows was open, and, tip-toeing up on the broad veranda, so that there would be no chance of the custodian hearing me, I entered a room through this window, and the whole silent house was at my disposal.

The interior would have struck a European unacquainted with Japan as being unfurnished, but I saw that it remained just as the Countess had left it. On a small table, standing about a foot from the floor, I saw a note similar to the one that had been handed to me when I first inquired at the gate, also three long slips of Japanese paper on which were written instructions in the Japanese language. I read them with amazement. The first said:

"This letter is to be given to a young man who calls, and who speaks Japanese and English."

On the next slip:

"This letter is to be given to an old man who speaks nothing but English."

The third slip bore:

"This is to be given to a young woman who speaks nothing but English."

There was also a minute description of Mr. Hemster, Miss Stretton, and myself, so that the man at the gate could make no mistake, which indeed he had not done. Hilda had not asked for a letter, therefore the remaining note had not been delivered.

Whoever concocted the plot had expected a search to be made for the House of the Million Blossoms, and of course knew that its situation could easily be found. I put all the documents into my pocket, and now went out by the public exit, greatly to the amazement of my urbane friend at the gate. I fear I may be accused of adopting Western methods, but the occasion seemed to me too serious for dilly-dallying. I pulled Mr. Hemster's revolver from my pocket and pointed it at the man's head.

"Now, you scoundrel," I said in his own tongue, "when did those women leave here? Answer me truly, or I shall take you prisoner to Nagasaki, where you will have to face the authorities."

I showed him the written instructions I had captured inside the house, and he saw at once that the game was up.

"Excellency!" said he, still politely enough, "I am but a poor man and a hireling. Many days ago a messenger brought me these instructions and three letters. No lady has been in this house for some years; the instructions were written by my mistress, the Countess, and I was compelled to follow them."

I saw that the man spoke the truth, and proceeded to cross-examine him on the motives which he imagined actuated this extraordinary complication; but he had told me all he knew, and was apparently as much in the dark regarding the motive as I was myself. I left him there, and hurried along the road over the hill to the spot where I had left Mr. Hemster and Hilda. Here I explained the conspiracy so far as I had discovered it, but the record of my investigation naturally did nothing to calm the fears of my employer, whose shrewdness had given a clue to the real situation at the House of the Million Blossoms. There was nothing to do but get back to Nagasaki as speedily as possible, and lay the case before the authorities. Hemster seemed suddenly to have become in truth an old man. We went directly to the hotel, and the clerk met us in the passage-way.

"Mr. Hemster," he said, "this telegram came for you about two hours ago."

The old gentleman tore open the envelope, read the dispatch, then crushed the paper in his hand.

"Just as I thought," he said. "She is in Seoul and

has found some way of communicating with me. Poor
little girl, poor little girl."

The father's voice broke momentarily, but he at once
pulled himself together again.

"Tremorne, tell the captain to get the yacht under
way. We will go on board immediately. We shall
want an escort from Chemulpo to Seoul; can we depend on getting them at the port as we did before, or
had we better bring them from Nagasaki?"

"I think, sir," said I, "that it would be well to take
a dozen from here. They are men I can trust, and I
shall have them aboard the yacht before steam is up."

"Very well," he said, decisively, "see to it."

I sent a messenger to the captain, then devoted all
my energies to the selecting of my twelve men, taking
care that they were properly armed and provided with
rations. I sent them aboard one by one or two by two
in sampans, so that too much attention might not be
attracted toward our expedition.

This task accomplished, I hurried back to the hotel,
and found Mr. Hemster and Hilda waiting for me.
Cammerford was there also, talking in a low voice very
earnestly with the old gentleman, who stood with his
eyes bent on the ground, making no reply to the other's
expostulations beyond shaking his head now and then.
Hilda and I went on ahead to the landing, the two men
following us. To my surprise Cammerford stepped
into the launch and continued talking to the silent man
beside him. When we reached the yacht Mr. Hemster
without a word mounted the steps to the deck. Hilda
followed, and Cammerford stood in the launch, a puz-

zled expression on his face. After a momentary hesitation he pushed past me, and ran up the steps. I also went on deck, and by the time I reached there my chief was already in his wicker chair with his feet on the rail, and a fresh unlit cigar in his mouth. Cammerford went jauntily up to him and said with a laugh that seemed somewhat forced:

"Well, Mr. Hemster, I propose to continue this discussion to Corea."

"Just as you please," replied the old man nonchalantly. "I think we can make you very comfortable on board."

CHAPTER XXIV

NOW it was full speed ahead and a direct line for Corea. Once in the open sea, we struck straight through the Archipelago and took our chances of running down an island, as the captain had said. There was no dawdling this time, for the engines were run to the top of their power. As was the case with our former voyages in these waters, the weather was perfect and the sea smooth.

Our dinner that night was on the whole a silent festival. The jovial captain did not come down, and Mr. Hemster sat moodily at the head of the table, absorbed in thought and doubtless tortured with anxiety. Cammerford was the only member of the party who endeavoured to make a show of cheerful demeanour. His manner with women was one of deferential urbanity, and, as he never ventured to joke with them, he was justly popular with the sex. I quite envied him his power of pleasing, which was so spontaneous that it seemed a natural and not an acquired gift. The man appeared to possess an almost hypnotic power over his fellow-creatures, and although I believed him to be one of the most untrustworthy rascals alive, yet I felt this belief crumbling away under the magnetic charm of his conversation.

A CHICAGO PRINCESS

The old gentleman at the head of the table was evidently immune so far as Cammerford's fascination was concerned. I surmised that there had come a hitch in the negotiations between them. There was no trace of uneasiness in Cammerford's attitude, and his voice was as mildly confident as ever. No one would guess that he was practically a self-invited guest at this board. Our host was completely taciturn, but the unbidden guest never risked a snub by addressing a direct question to him, although he airily included Mr. Hemster with the rest of us within the area of his polite discourse. Hilda was scarcely more responsive than Mr. Hemster and seemed troubled because he was troubled, and as I possessed an instinctive dislike for Cammerford it will be seen that he had a most difficult rôle to play, which he enacted with a success that would have done credit to Sir Henry Irving himself. If there was indeed, as I suspected, a conflict between the elder man and the younger, I found myself wondering which would win, but such a quiet atmosphere of confidence enwrapped the latter that I began to fear Mr. Hemster had met his match, in spite of the fact that he held all the trump cards. Cammerford represented the new school of financiers, who juggled with billions as a former generation had played with millions. My sympathies were entirely with Mr. Hemster, but if I had been a sporting man my bet would have been laid on Cammerford. I mention this as an instance of the hypnotic power I have referred to. I knew that Cammerford could not form his gigantic trust and leave Mr. Hemster out; therefore, as I say, the elder man held the trumps. Nevertheless the bearing of Cammerford indicated such reserved assurance that I felt certain he would ultimately bend the old man to his will, and I watched for the result of this opposition of forces with the eagerness with which one awaits the climax of an exciting play on the stage.

After dinner Hilda came on deck for half an hour or thereabouts, and we walked up and down together. The excitement of the day and the uncertainty that lay ahead of us had told heavily on the poor girl, and I had not the heart to persuade her to remain longer on deck. She was rather depressed and admittedly weary of the life we were leading. So I took cowardly advantage of this and proposed we should get married at the American Consulate as soon as the yacht returned to Nagasaki. Then, I said, we could make our way to Yokohama and take passage on a regular liner for San Francisco.

To this proposal she made no reply, but walked demurely by my side with downcast eyes.

" Think of the glories of Chicago at this moment! " I cried enthusiastically, wishing to appeal to the home feeling. " Dinner finished; the roar of the traffic in the streets; the brilliancy of the electric light; the theatres open, and the gay crowds entering therein. Let us make for Chicago."

She looked up at me with a wan little smile, and laughed quietly.

" You *do* need a guardian, as Papa Hemster says. I suppose it is about noon in Chicago at the present moment, and I don't see why the theatres should be

290

open at that hour. It is the roar of the wheat pit, and not of the traffic you are hearing. I fear your visit to Chicago was of the briefest, for your picture is not very convincing. Still, I confess I wish I were there now, if you were with me." Then with a slight sigh she added, " I 'll accept that guardianship at Nagasaki. Good-night, my dear," and with that she whisked away and disappeared before I was aware of her meditated escape.

I lit a fresh cigar and continued my promenade alone. As I walked aft I caught snatches of the musical monotone of Cammerford's voice. Ever since dinner time he had been in earnest conversation with Mr. Hemster, who sat in his usual chair at the stern of the boat. So far as I am aware, Mr. Hemster was leaving the burden of the talk to the younger man, who, from the tone of his voice, seemed in deadly earnest. At last Mr. Hemster got up and threw his cigar overboard. I heard him say:

" I told you, Mr. Cammerford, that I would not discuss this matter further until I reached Nagasaki. The papers are all in my desk under lock and key in the room at the hotel, and that room is closed and sealed. I 'll say no more about this scheme until I am back there."

" And when you are back there, Mr. Hemster, what action are you going to take? "

" Whatever action seems to be best for my own interests, Mr. Cammerford."

" Well, from most men that reply would be very unsatisfactory. However, I am glad to say I trust you completely, Mr. Hemster, and I know you will do the square thing in the end."

"I'm glad you think so," said the old man curtly, as he went down the stairway. Cammerford stood there for a few moments, then strode forward and joined me.

"May I beg a light of you?" he asked, as if he were conferring a favour.

I don't care to light one cigar from another, so I struck a match and held it while he took advantage of the flame.

"Thanks. Now, Tremorne, I want to talk with you as to a friend. We were friends once, you know."

"True; the kind of friend the celebrated phrase refers to, perhaps."

"What phrase?"

"'God protect me from my friends,' or words to that effect."

He laughed most genially.

"That's one on me," he said. "However, I look on our score as being wiped out. Can't you let bygones be bygones?"

"Oh, yes."

"You see you are in a way responsible. I have turned over the money to you. Granted I was forced to do so. I claim no merit in the matter, but I do say a bargain is a bargain. I showed you the old man's letter to me, in which he said if I did thus and so by you, he would join me in the big beef combine. You remember that, don't you?"

" Naturally, I should n't soon forget it, or forget the generosity of Mr. Hemster in writing it."

" Oh, generosity is cheap when you are doing it at somebody else's expense. Still, I don't complain of that at all. What I say is this: I've kept my part of the contract strictly and honestly, but now the old man is trying to euchre me."

" I remember also, Mr. Cammerford, that you said Mr. Hemster was a rogue or dishonest, or something of like effect."

" Well, so he is."

" In that case, why do you object to being euchred by him?"

" Well, you see, I had his promise in writing, and I thought I was safe."

" You have it in writing still, I presume. If he does not live up to what he has written, you probably have your recourse at law, for they say there is no wrong without a remedy."

"Oh, that's all talking through your hat. It is n't a lawsuit I'm after, but the co-operation of Mr. Hemster. What chance would I have against a man of his wealth?"

" I 'm sure I don't know. What is it you wish from me? Advice?"

" I wanted to explain the situation that has arisen, and I wish to know if you have anything to suggest that will lead the old man to do the square thing?"

" I have no suggestion to make, Mr. Cammerford."

" Supposing he does not keep his promise, don't you

think it would be fair that the money I expended on the strength of it should be returned to me?"

"It does seem reasonable, I admit."

"I am glad to hear you say so, and to tell the truth, Mr. Tremorne, it is just the action I should expect of you."

"What action?"

"The returning of the money, of course."

"Bless my soul, you don't suppose I'm going to return a penny of it, do you?"

"Ah, your honesty is theory then, not practice."

"My dear sir, my honesty is both theory and practice. The money is mine. I made you no promises regarding it. In fact, I refused to make any promise when you offered me half the amount. If I had made any engagements I should have kept them."

"I see. I take it then you do not regard yourself as bound by any promises the old man made on your behalf?"

"Certainly not. I knew nothing of the matter until you showed me his letter."

"Your position is perfectly sound, Mr. Tremorne, and I unreservedly withdraw the imputation I put upon your honesty a moment since. But the truth is that this amount represents a very serious loss to me. It was a sprat thrown out to catch a whale, or, rather, a whale thrown out to catch a shoal of whales. But if I lose the whale and do not catch my shoal, then I have done a very bad piece of business by coming East. Through this proposed combine I expected to make several millions. Now, if you will join in with me, and put

294

your half-million into the pool, I 'll guarantee that before a month you have doubled it."

" You gave me a chance like that once before, Mr. Cammerford."

The man laughed heartily as if I had perpetrated a very amusing joke.

" Oh, yes, but that was years ago. We have both learned a good deal since."

" I certainly have, Mr. Cammerford. I have learned so much that I will not part with a penny of the money; not a red cent of it, as we say out West. That sum is going to be safely salted down, and it 's not going to be salted in a corned-beef tub either. I don't mind telling you that I intend to get married upon it at the American Consulate at Nagasaki before a week is past."

" Really? Allow me to congratulate you, my boy. I surmised that was the way the land lay, and I quite envy you your charming young lady."

" Thanks ! "

" But you see, Mr. Tremorne, that makes your money doubly safe. I noticed that Mr. Hemster is as fond of Miss Stretton as he is of his own daughter, and if you give me the half million, he 'll see to it that you make a hundred per cent on it."

" I don't at all agree with you, Mr. Cammerford. To speak with brutal frankness, if I trusted you with the money which you once succeeded in detaching from me,—if I trusted you with it again,—he would merely look upon me as a hopeless fool, and I must say I think he would be right."

John C. Cammerford was a man whom you could n't

insult: it was not business to take offence, so he took none, but merely laughed again in his free-hearted way.

" The old man thinks I don't see what his game is, but I do. He is playing for time. He expects to hold me out here in the East, dangling this bait before me, until it is too late for me to do anything with my options. Now, he is going to get left at that game. I have more cards up my sleeve than he imagines, but I don't want to have any trouble with him: I want to deal with him in a friendly manner for our mutual benefit. I 'll play fair if he plays fair. It is n't too much to ask a man to keep his word, is it ! "

" No, the demand does n't appear excessive."

" Very good. Now, I wish you would have a quiet talk with him. I can see that he reposes great confidence in you. You have admitted that my request is an honest one, so I hope you won't mind just presenting my side of the case to him."

" It is none of my business, Mr. Cammerford. I could not venture to take such a liberty with Mr. Hemster."

" But you admit the old man is n't playing fair ? "

" I admit nothing of the sort: I don't know his side of the story at all. He may have reasons for declining to deal with you, which seem to him conclusive."

" Granted. But nevertheless, don't you think he should return the money given on the strength of his promise ? "

" Really I would rather not discuss the matter any

further, Mr. Cammerford, if you don't mind. I overheard you telling him at the head of the companion-way that you trusted him completely. Very well, then, why not continue to do so?"

Cammerford gave a short laugh that had little of mirth in it: his politeness was evidently becoming worn threadbare, and I imagine he was inwardly cursing my obstinacy. There was silence between us for several minutes, then he said sharply:

"Is this yarn about the kidnapping of his daughter all guff?"

"Who told you about it?" I asked.

"Oh, he did: gave that as the reason he did n't wish to talk business."

"The story is true, and I think the reason is valid. If you take my advice, you will not talk business with him in the face of his prohibition until his mind is at rest regarding his daughter."

"Well, I guess I 'll take your advice; it seems to be the only thing I 'm going to get out of you. I thought the daughter story was only a yarn to bluff me from coming aboard the yacht."

"It was n't, and furthermore, I don't think you showed your usual perspicacity in not accepting Mr. Hemster's intimation that he did n't want to be bothered at this particular time."

"Oh, well, as to that," said Cammerford, confidently, "the old man has been making a monkey of me for some weeks now, and the whole matter might have been settled in as many hours if he had cared to do so. He is n't going to shake me off so easily as he thinks.

297

I 'll stick to him till he keeps his promise, and don't you forget it."

" All right, I 'll endeavour to keep it in mind."

" You won't be persuaded to try and lure him on to the straight and narrow path of honesty, Mr. Tremorne?"

" No, I 'm not sure that he 's off it. I have always found him treading that path."

" I see. Well, good-night. When do we reach that outlandish place,—whatever its name is?"

" We ought to arrive at Chemulpo some time to-morrow night."

" Chemulpo, is it? Well, I wish it was Chicago. So long."

" Good-night," I responded, and with that he left the world to darkness and to me.

CHAPTER XXV

WE came to anchor a little after ten the next night. Mr. Hemster was naturally very impatient, and wished to proceed at once to the capital, but the customs authorities refused to let us land until daylight. Cammerford talked very valiantly of forcing our way ashore and going to Seoul in the darkness in spite of all opposition, and indeed the old gentleman was rather in favour of such a course; but I pointed out that our mission might be one of great delicacy, and that it was as well not to use force unless we were compelled to do so.

"Even in New York," said I, "we should not be allowed to proceed up the harbour after sunset, no matter how anxious we might be to land."

This was not thought to be a parallel case, but the old gentleman suggested that, as he wished no undue publicity, it would be better to wait until daylight and make our landing with as little ostentation as possible. I tried bribery, but for once it was ineffective, and in spite of the fact that I incurred the contempt of the energetic Cammerford, I counselled less hurry and more speed, though there was nothing to do but turn in and get a night's sleep in preparation for the toilsome journey in the morning.

I was on deck at daylight and found my Japs had all

299

disappeared except their leader. He explained to me that he thought it best to get them ashore during the night unobtrusively in sampans. They would be waiting for us, he said, two or three miles beyond the port on the Seoul road. Now our Excellencies might disembark, he added, without attracting any attention. I complimented the little man on his forethought, and, sure enough, we found our company just where he said we would.

The next surprise was that Cammerford also had disappeared. I went down to his stateroom, but found his bed had not been slept in. The Japs had seen nothing of him, neither had any of the crew, so our unbidden guest had departed as he came.

Hilda was evidently most reluctant to take the journey. She told me she had seen enough of Seoul to last her a lifetime, but as she found that Mr. Hemster was most anxious for her to accompany us, she did what she always had done, and sacrificed her own inclinations in deference to the wishes of others.

We had got nearly half way to Seoul when I saw with alarm a large party, apparently of Corean soldiers, marching westward. They were easily ten to one as compared with our escort, yet I had not the slightest doubt our Japs would put them all to flight if they attempted to bar our way. Taking two of the Japs with me, I galloped on ahead to learn the intentions of the cavalcade in front. They paused in their march on seeing us coming up, and their leader galloped forward to meet me. To my surprise I saw it was the Prime Minister himself.

"Well, you old scoundrel," I cried, "your head is still on your shoulders unfortunately. What's the meaning of this movement of troops. Do you think you're going to stop us?"

"Oh, no, Excellency, no. I have come to greet you, and offer you the profound regard of the Emperor himself."

"Now, just try to speak the truth for once; it won't hurt you. You know very well that you had no word of our coming."

"Pardon, most Gracious Excellency, but your white ambassador arrived as soon as the gates were open this morning."

"Our white ambassador! Oh, that's Cammerford, very likely. So he has reached the capital, has he?"

"Yes, Excellency, and has received the honour due."

"That ought to be a gorgeous reception. And did he send you to meet us?"

"No, Excellency, it was the white Princess."

"Ah, you villain, you did kidnap her after all. Now if any harm has come to her, off goes your head, and down goes your pasteboard city."

"Ah, Excellency," said the Prime Minister with a wail of woe, "it was indeed depths of wickedness, but what was I to do? If I did not bring her to Seoul, not only was my head lost, but the heads of all my kin; and now, alas, the Emperor says that if she goes not willingly away he will yet execute me, and all my family as well. Excellency, it was an unlucky day when the white Princess came to the Palace. The Emperor is in fear of his life, and terror reigns in every corner. Yet she would not go until the King, her father, brought his war-ship to Chemulpo, and she demanded to be escorted by the whole court with the honours of an Empress from the capital to the sea. She was going to make the Emperor himself come, but he bowed his forehead in the dust, a thing unknown these ten thousand years in Corea, and so she laughed at him and allowed him to remain in the Palace. She has made a mock of his Majesty and his ancestors."

"Serves him jolly well right," said I, beginning to get an inkling of how the case stood. "Her ancestors fought for liberty, and it is not likely she is going to be deprived of hers by any tan-bark monarch who foolishly undertakes the job. Is the lady still at the Palace, Hun Woe?"

"No, Excellency, she is on her way hither, escorted by the Court, and riding proudly with her white ambassador. Indeed," he continued, looking over his shoulder, "I can see them now, coming over the brow of that hill. She was so anxious to meet her father that she would not await your coming."

"All right, Hun Woe, you line up your troops on each side of the road, and see that they bow low when the Princess passes. I shall return and acquaint the King, her father, with the state of the poll."

So saying I wheeled my horse, galloped back, and informed the old gentleman that everything was all right. He heaved a deep sigh of relief, and I fancied his eyes twinkled somewhat as I related what particulars I had gathered of the reign of terror in Seoul since his daughter's enforced arrival.

By the time I had finished my recital the cavalcade to the rear had passed between the lines of prostrate soldiers. The old gentleman moved forward to meet his daughter, and she came galloping on her pony and greeted him with an affectionate abandon that was delightful to see, although when she flung her arms round his neck she nearly unhorsed him. Her reception of the rest of us was like that of a school-girl out on a lark. She seemed to regard her abduction as the greatest fun that ever was, and was bubbling with laughter and glee. She kissed the sedate Hilda as if she were an only sister, reproaching herself that even for a moment she had preferred that little beast of a Countess, as she called her, to so noble a treasure as Miss Stretton. To me she was as gracious as if I were her dearest friend.

"And now, Poppa," she cried, "shall I make this circus come with us to Chemulpo? I can do what I please with them; they belong to me."

"I don't think we want that crowd tagging after us, Gertie," said her father without enthusiasm.

"Then, Mr. Tremorne," she said, "will you order them home again, and tell 'em to be good for ever after. And oh! I want you to ask the Prime Minister if I did n't make that old Emperor kow-tow to me."

"He has already admitted that you did, Miss Hemster."

"Then that's all right: I thought they'd try to deny it."

A CHICAGO PRINCESS

I bade an affectionate farewell to Hun Woe, who was as glad to be quit of me as I was to be rid of him, and we have never seen each other since.

I don't remember ever taking part in a jollier excursion than that which now set forth towards Chemulpo, which place we reached before sunset.

Miss Hemster related her adventures with a gusto and enjoyment that I never saw equalled. Even her father smiled now and then at the exuberant humour of her declamation. It seemed that the Countess was in the pay of the Corean Government, probably as a spy. The Prime Minister had telegraphed her to win the confidence of Miss Hemster if she could, and so the Countess had made application to the American Consul and succeeded even beyond her fondest hopes. There had been no intention of going to the House of the Million Blossoms, but she had proposed instead to Miss Hemster a round of visits among the nobility of Japan, or at least whatever section of them lived near Nagasaki. As this round was to take some time, and as the Countess proclaimed that it must be done in strict secrecy, she outlined the writing of the different letters which her caretaker at the villa would hand to whoever called, if an investigation was made, as the wily Countess thought was highly probable, and this scheme proved peculiarly attractive to Miss Hemster and was accordingly carried out, and the young lady laughed till tears came into her eyes when I told her how I had been deceived by the receipt of my letter.

After landing from the yacht the Countess took Miss Hemster and her maid to a tea house situated on the shore of the bay, and from the moment they drank tea there, Miss Hemster and her maid remembered nothing more until they found themselves on board the Chinese steamer.

" Did you know about the attempted sinking of the yacht? " I asked.

" I was n't sure," she said. " I was in a sort of daze: I seemed to have awakened when they began to take up the anchor, but I was stupid and headachy. Then there came a crash, and I screamed fit to kill, but those Chinese brutes put us into the cabin, and after that of course there was no escape. We did not land at Chemulpo, but somewhere along the coast. It was a fearful ride into Seoul, but after that I had my revenge; I made the old Emperor and his Court stand around, I tell you, for I had a revolver and plenty of cartridges in my trunk, and once I got them the situation belonged to me."

" And where are your trunks, Gertie? " asked her practical father.

" Oh, they 're stored in Chemulpo. The Emperor wanted me to leave, but I would n't until you came and I was provided with a proper escort. He wanted me to go back on the same old Chinese tub, but I told him I 'd a steamer of my own coming."

We got the trunks and set sail for Nagasaki once more. The voyage was a dream of delight. Never did I see Miss Gertrude Hemster, or any one else for that matter, so admirably charming and considerate of everyone around her. Mr. Cammerford proved a most devoted cavalier, and this gave Hilda and me opportunity for converse which we did not neglect. Gertrude Hemster cheered her father's heart by telling him that she was tired of king-hunting and wanted to get back to Chicago. When we arrived at Nagasaki I made arrangements for our marriage at the American Consulate. Miss Hemster was most fascinatingly sweet to Hilda when she heard the news. We all went together to the consulate, Cammerford asking permission to join our party. When we arrived, Cammerford, who seemed to be taking a great deal upon himself, said politely to the Consul:

"I should think a real American wedding takes precedence over an international affair, but at any rate I bespoke your services first."

The Consul smiled and said such was indeed the case; then, to the amazement of Hilda and myself, Gertrude, with a laugh, took the outstretched hand of John C. Cammerford and stood before the official, who married them according to the laws of the land to which they belonged.

"What do you think of this combine, Mr. Hemster?" said Cammerford with his most engaging smile, holding out his hand to his newly made father-in-law.

The old man took it and said quietly:

"Whoever makes Gertie happy makes me content."

Next came the turn of Hilda and myself.

THE END